Endeavor

⑤

New Readers Press
A Publishing Division of ProLiteracy

The following teachers participated in pilot testing of Endeavor:

Evelyn Surma, Adult Education Teacher
Anaheim Union High School District, Anaheim, CA

Maria Pagnotta, ABE-GED Professor
Seminole Community College, Sanford, FL

Rachel M. Slavkin, Adjunct Faculty
Seminole Community College, Sanford, FL

Lora Zangari, Professional Development Coordinator
Lancaster Lebanon IU13, Lancaster, PA

Endeavor 5
ISBN 978-1-56420-855-2

Copyright © 2009 New Readers Press
New Readers Press
A Publishing Division of ProLiteracy
1320 Jamesville Avenue, Syracuse, New York 13210
www.newreaderspress.com

Printed in the United States of America
9 8 7 6 5 4 3 2

All proceeds from the sale of New Readers Press materials support literacy programs in the United States and worldwide.

Contributing Author: Vista Resources, Inc.
Developmental Editors: Ellen Northcutt, Donna Townsend
Creative Director: Andrea Woodbury
Production Specialist: Maryellen Casey
Art and Design Supervisor: James P. Wallace
Illustrator: Kathleen Rietz, represented by Wilkinson Studios, Inc.

Contents

Choosing Happiness

Learning Objectives

In this lesson you will:

▨ Learn about how people can make themselves happier.

▨ Learn to draw conclusions.

▨ Master the key vocabulary used in the article.

▨ Write suggestions for being happier.

Key Vocabulary

anxious *(adjective)* worried, nervous

concentrate *(verb)* to give one's attention to

conflicts *(noun)* strong differences of opinion

dwell on *(verb)* to think about something a lot of the time

habits *(noun)* usual ways of behaving

leisure *(noun)* time free from work

negative *(adjective)* not positive; bad

poverty *(noun)* the state of being poor

recognizing *(verb)* understanding or realizing

relationships *(noun)* connections of some kind

Before You Read

Be an active reader. Think about what you want to learn from this article about ways to be happy. Ask yourself questions and look for the answers.

Set a purpose for reading.

1. What do you think you will learn from this article?

   _____

   _____

   _____

2. How could reading this article help make your life better?

   _____

   _____

   _____

   _____

Ask yourself questions.

1. Am I happy now? Why or why not?

   _____

   _____

   _____

   _____

2. Could I be happier? How would that change my life?

   _____

   _____

   _____

   _____

   _____

How To Be Happy

Read this article to find out how to be happy. Highlight the sentences that tell different ways to be happy.

Everyone wants to be happy. For many years, people thought that happiness was something you either had or you didn't. Today, though, that view is changing. Now many people think that you can make changes in your life that will make you happier. You can choose to be happy.

5   Part of being happy, it turns out, is external . That is, happiness is caused by conditions outside of you rather than inside. For example, one proven way to make yourself happier is to exercise. When you run hard or play sports, you feel less depressed and **anxious.**

What you do during the rest of your day can make you happy, too. Some
10 people are lucky enough to have jobs they love. Research shows that when people are completely involved in what they do, they lose track of time and feel satisfied. But not all people love their jobs. Many like their jobs, but are not completely involved in them. Luckily there are other ways to find happiness.

15   In your free time, you can participate in activities that make you happy. Find something you love to do in your **leisure** time. Many people think watching TV makes them happy. Researchers found, though, that TV watching creates some of the lowest levels of happiness. When people watch TV, they aren't really involved. They aren't using their minds and bodies to
20 challenge themselves. So instead of watching TV, find active things that make you happy and do them.

Many people who are happy have **habits** of mind that help them. They train themselves to be happy. One way to do that is to make a point of being

external (adjective)
outside of something
or someone

researchers (noun)
people who collect
information and study
about something

psychologists (noun)
   people who deal with
   the science of the mind

25 grateful. You may have bad things in your life, but you also have good things. Focus on those. Some psychologists ask their patients to think of something that they are grateful for every day. That gets people to **concentrate** on the good things and steers them toward happiness.

1. What is an external way to feel happier?

   _____

   _____

2. Does watching TV make you happy? Explain.

   _____

   _____

3. How do you think being grateful can help make you happy?

   _____

   _____

Keep on reading to find out other ways to keep yourself happy. Highlight those ways as you read.

✓   People who are happy also forgive others. People who remain angry are doing themselves no good. That anger turns to bitterness. Walking around 30 with a load of bitterness can keep you from being happy.
   Instead, practice forgiveness. Think about why you are angry or hurt. Try to understand what happened from the point of view of the person who hurt you. Be generous. Think of a time when someone forgave you. Finally, forgive the other person. You can write a letter or you can tell him or her in person. You 35 can even write a letter to yourself.
   Another good habit of mind is to get rid of **negative** thoughts. There are ways you can train yourself to do that. Most of these ways have to do with **recognizing** that a thought is negative, and then dealing with it. Some people use meditation . When you meditate, you recognize that a negative thought is 40 in your head. Then you let it go right through your mind. You don't **dwell on** it.

meditation (noun)
   a way of calming or
   relaxing the mind

4. Write some ideas about how to practice forgiveness.

   _____

   _____

   _____

   _____

Finish reading the article to find more tips for making yourself happy. Highlight those tips as you read.

Some people are sure that the only thing they need to make themselves happy is money. After all, worrying about money can really make people unhappy. Many of us think if only we had enough money for that car, we would be happy. What research shows, though, is that after you have enough money
45 to keep you out of **poverty,** more money doesn't bring happiness. More stuff doesn't make us happy. Once you have that car, you may be happy for a little while. But soon, you will get used to the car. Then you may think a bigger or better car will make you happy.

What can make people happy are their **relationships.** Studies show that
50 close friends make people happy. Those friends are there to share good times. They are also there to get you through bad times and keep you from feeling unhappy for very long. So—make friends. Find someone who shares your interests. Ask him to play basketball or ask her to go out for coffee. Having a group of friends can be one of the best ways to stay happy.

55 Being married can also make people happy. In study after study, the happiest people are married. They tend to live longer, too.

Of course marriage isn't always easy. Being married can often mean working through **conflicts.** That can be hard work. Couples who fight may be as happy as those who don't fight. It turns out everybody fights. If you want to be happy
60 in your marriage, marry someone who is a friend. The happiest people, both men and women, said they were great friends with their spouses.

There is hope. You can be happy. What's more, you can make yourself happier. You can find an activity you like. You can pay attention to happy thoughts. You can make friends. It turns out that being happy is something you
65 can choose to be.

5. Do you think that having more money would make you happy? Why or why not?

_____

_____

_____

_____

6. How can having friends help make you happy?

_____

_____

_____

_____

After You Read

Happy - joyful, cheerful, merry, contented, satisfied

Build a robust vocabulary. *opposite - sad*

Writing Sentences   Write a complete sentence to respond to each of the following questions or statements. Use the underlined word in your answer. Use the definitions on page 5 to help you.

1. What do you like to do in your <u>leisure</u> time?

    _____

2. What are two <u>habits</u> of mind that can make a person happy?

    _____

3. What are some issues that married people might have <u>conflicts</u> about?

    _____

4. Who do you have good <u>relationships</u> with?

    _____

5. Tell how you feel when you <u>concentrate</u>.

    _____

Sentence Completions   Complete each sentence using a word from the box.

anxious	concentrate	conflicts	dwell on	habits
leisure	negative	poverty	recognizing	relationships

mental distress, uneasiness because of fear or danger; greatly uneasy

1. Jill slept poorly because she was _anxious_____ about her test the next day.

2. Please don't _____ bad thoughts.

3. _____ that a thought is bothering you allows you to let that thought go.

4. _____ is an international problem.

5. Thinking *I hate him!* is a _____ thought.

Word Building   A **root word** is a base from which other words are formed. Letters are added before and/or after the root word to form a new word. Look at the following sentence from the article.

> They are also there to get you through bad times and keep you from feeling unhappy for very long.

Three words in the sentence have been formed from root words: *times, feeling,* and *unhappy.* Circle the root word in each of those words. Check your answers with a partner.

doubtful	watching	researcher	unfriendly	forgiveness

Look at the words above. Can you find the root word in each of them? Write the root words below. Then use each word in a sentence. The first one is done for you.

1. doubtful: _doubt_

   They were doubtful that they could afford a new car.

2. watching: _____

   _____

3. researcher: _____

   _____

4. unfriendly: _____

   _____

5. forgiveness: _____

   _____

Writing Activity   Write a short paragraph that correctly uses key vocabulary words to tell how to be happy. Use at least four of the words from the list on page 5. Reread the definitions, if necessary.

_____

_____

_____

_____

Think about your reading.

Check your comprehension.   Answer each question. If you don't know the answer, reread the lines in parentheses.

1. Why isn't watching TV likely to make people happy? (lines 18–20)

   _____

2. How can forgiving others make you happy? (lines 28–30)

   _____

3. Why won't a new car make you happy for long? (lines 46–47)

   _____

Use reading skills: Draw conclusions.

When you **draw a conclusion,** you add information you read to information you already know. For example, every married couple you know has conflicts. Then you read that being married means learning to work through conflicts and that married people tend to be happier. You can draw the conclusion that marriage, even with its conflicts, can help people be happier.

Draw conclusions. In the second paragraph of the article, you learn about external ways people make themselves happy, such as playing sports. You know that you take your dog for a walk every morning and every evening. You can draw the conclusion, based on what you read and what you know, that walking your dog helps make you happy.

Reread this section of the article about being happy:

> Researchers found, though, that TV watching creates some of the lowest levels of happiness. When people watch TV, they aren't really involved. They aren't using their minds and bodies to challenge themselves.

1. What did you learn from reading about TV and happiness?

   _____

2. What do you know from your own experience watching TV and your own happiness?

   _____

3. What conclusion can you draw about how much TV you should watch to make yourself happy?

   _____

   _____

Use a graphic organizer.
When you draw a conclusion, you take information from what you read and relate it to your own experiences. Look at the information in the boxes labeled *What you read* and *What you know.*

What You Read	**What You Know**
Close friends make people happy.	I have a lot of close friends.

Draw a Conclusion

Write About It

Write suggestions for becoming happier.

The article tells things you can do to make yourself happier. Imagine you are giving advice to an unhappy friend. Write a paragraph that talks about things your friend might do to be happier. Use the article as a guide.

Prewriting   In the ovals below, write four suggestions that your friend can use to be happier. This will help you organize your thinking and your writing.

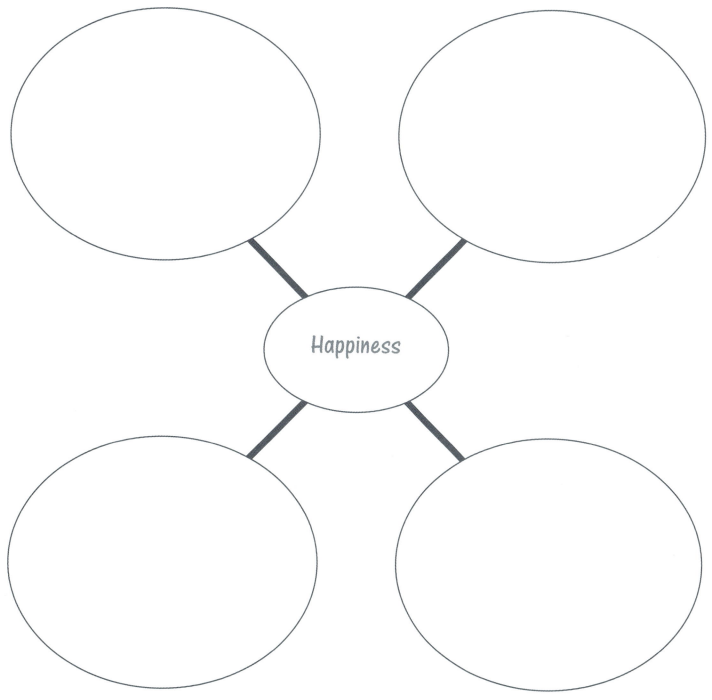

Thinking Beyond Reading   Explain the suggestions you wrote in your graphic organizer to a partner. Have your partner ask questions about what you wrote. Add ideas to your graphic organizer to help make your suggestions easier to understand. Then do the same for your partner. Here are some possible questions to ask your partner:

- What are some things a person can do to be happier?

- If a person does all the things you suggest, what do you think will happen?

Write a draft.   Write a first draft of a paragraph that describes ways your friend can increase his or her happiness. First explain what you are trying to do. Then describe each action the person would need to take. Base your writing on what you know about your friend and on the ideas in your idea map on page 13. Your last sentence should describe the result of following your suggestions.

_____

_____

_____

_____

_____

_____

_____

_____

_____

_____

_____

_____

_____

Revise and create a final draft.   Write your final draft on a separate piece of paper. As you revise, check your draft for these points:

- Did you start by explaining the purpose of the paragraph?

- Did you include suggestions of ways to be happier?

- Did you check spelling and grammar to make sure your writing is clear and correct?

Getting the Job

Learning Objectives

In this lesson you will:

■ Learn about how to get a job.

■ Learn to identify main idea and details.

■ Master the key vocabulary used in the article.

■ Write a thank-you letter to a job interviewer.

Key Vocabulary

application *(noun)* a form filled out by a person who wants a job

confident *(adjective)* feeling sure of oneself

current *(adjective)* right now

experience *(noun)* understanding or skills gained from practice or an earlier activity

impression *(noun)* the effect that a person has on someone

opportunity *(noun)* a chance to do something

positive *(adjective)* good, favorable

previous *(adjective)* coming before, earlier

promoted *(verb)* got a better job at the same workplace

reliable *(adjective)* dependable

Before You Read

When you read the article, think about what you already know about job interviewing. Set a purpose for your reading, and ask yourself an active reading question: How might this article prepare me for my next job interview?

Set a purpose for reading.

THINK ABOUT IT

1. What do you expect to learn from reading this article?

   _____

   _____

   _____

   _____

I'm not sure I ever gave much thought to getting ready for a job interview. It makes sense to think about it ahead of time, though. That might help me have a better interview.

2. How might this article help you in your life?

   _____

   _____

   _____

   _____

Ask yourself questions as you read.

THINK ABOUT IT

1. As I read about getting references, I wonder who might be a good reference for me. (List the names of two or three people.)

   _____

   _____

   _____

If I were the interviewer, I wonder what questions I would ask to make sure the person was a good fit for the job.

2. The article tells me to follow up with a thank-you letter. What should I say in a thank-you letter? (List some things you might say.)

   _____

   _____

   _____

   _____

The Job Interview

Read this article to find out how to get a job you want. Highlight or mark the ideas you think will help you most.

Before you get the job, there is the job interview . Many people think talking to a possible employer is a bit scary. We all have to go through it, though. No one gets a job without it. It doesn't matter what kind of job you are after. It could be in a factory, a restaurant, an office, or outdoors. All
5   employers want to talk to the person they will be hiring.

Prepare questions and answers.

One of the best ways to keep from getting nervous about a job interview is to get ready for it. Start by learning what you can about the company. Then think about what you might be asked at the interview. You will be asked why
10   you want the job. You may be asked why you would be good for the job. Think about your **experience.** How does it make you a good fit for the job? If you have no job experience, think about skills you have that would interest an employer.

Another popular question is "What are your strengths and weaknesses?" Come up with a true answer that makes you someone the interviewer wants
15   to hire. For example, one of your strengths may be that you work well with others. When telling about a weakness, try to think of a way that the weakness could work to the employer's advantage. For example, trying too hard to do a good job may be one of your weaknesses. But an employer might find this to be a good trait for an employee to have.
20   The interviewer will be making a judgment about how you would fit into the business. He or she will try to figure out if you will be a hard worker. Are you **reliable?** Will you show up for work on time?

job interview (noun)
   a face-to-face meeting to question someone looking for a job

employer (noun)
   a company or person who hires people to do work

You can also come up with questions to ask your interviewer. You can
ask what you will be doing and what the hours are. You might want to ask
25 if there is a chance to grow and get **promoted.** Ask questions that show
you know about the business. Stay away from questions such as "What does
your company do?" That shows the interviewer that you haven't done your
homework. Also, don't ask about how much you will make. If you are offered a
job, ask then.

1. What are some questions you might ask an employer?

    _____

    _____

Keep reading to find out what to do at the interview. Highlight or mark the
ideas you think are most useful.

30 **Plan for the interview.**
    Plan what you will wear to the interview. Be sure your clothes are neat and
clean. Don't wear jeans, sneakers, shorts, a t-shirt, or a sweatshirt. You may be
applying for a job with a landscaper or in a factory. You still want to make a
good **impression** on the interviewer by dressing nicely.

35 Come to the interview prepared. Often, you will be asked to fill out an
application first. If you have the information with you, it won't take a lot of
time to fill out. Bring your social security card and a résumé or a listing of
your work history. Have contact information for three references handy.
These should be people who know you and have worked with you. An old
40 boss who likes you is a good choice. Check with these people before you tell
an interviewer to call them. If you have no work experience, your references
may be friends or teachers, but not relatives. Be sure these people will say good
things about your character and work ethic .

Make arrangements to spend as much time at the interview as needed. If
45 you have a job, don't try to schedule your interview during a lunch break. If
the interview goes longer than expected you would be returning late to your
current job. It is better to take a half-day or full day off. Do not bring your
children to the interview. If you cannot get day care, call the employer and ask
to change the interview to another day.

50 **Complete the interview.**
    Arrive early. That will give you time to take a deep breath, to check your
hair, and to straighten your clothes. It's important that the first impression you
make is a good one. Hold out your hand with a smile. Look the interviewer in
the eye. Show him or her that you are **confident** and excited about the job.
55 Take care not to fidget or gaze around the room.

résumé (noun)
    a person's work history,
    qualifications

references (noun)
    people who will
    tell how well you
    performed in a job

work ethic (noun)
    a person's work habits,
    such as being on time

Once you sit down, follow the lead of the interviewer. Let him or her talk first. Listen carefully, and answer questions politely and completely. Don't talk on and on or take over the conversation. If the interviewer asks if you have any questions, ask the ones you have ready. If you sense that the interviewer is getting impatient, stop. Be careful, too, with how you talk. This is no time to use slang or bad grammar.

2. What are some ways to act during the interview?

_____

_____

Finish reading the article to find out more about how to get the job.

The interviewer will most likely ask about the jobs you have had. That can be tricky if your experience wasn't a good one. Even so, tell about the jobs you have had in **positive** terms. Tell what you liked about them. Tell how what you learned will help you in this new job. Never say something bad about a **previous** employer. If this is your first job, be sure the interviewer knows that. Talk about how this job will be a good **opportunity** for you starting out.

As you finish the interview, shake the interviewer's hand again. Thank him or her. Explain why you would be perfect for the job. Review what you have to offer. Make sure you have the interviewer's name, phone number, e-mail address, and mailing address. That way, you can contact him or her later.

Thank the interviewer.

There is more to do after the interview. You will impress the person doing the hiring by writing a thank-you letter or e-mail. Make sure you address the letter or e-mail to the person who talked to you. Tell why you would be a good hire. If you can, make a point of talking about something from the interview. Explain what you did at earlier jobs and tell how you might do the same thing at the new job.

Remember, though, that a job interview is not a one-way street. You may need a job, but the person hiring has needs, too. If you show you are the perfect person for the job, nobody will be happier than the interviewer.

3. What is the most important thing you learned about having a good job interview?

_____

_____

_____

After You Read

Build a robust vocabulary.

Writing Sentences   Write a complete sentence to respond to each of the following questions. Use the underlined word in your answer. Use the definitions on page 15 to help you.

1. How has your <u>experience</u> helped you get a job?

    _____

2. What can you do to feel <u>positive</u> about a job interview?

    _____

3. How can you make a good first <u>impression</u> in an interview?

    _____

4. How would you prove you are <u>reliable</u>?

    _____

5. What is something you are <u>confident</u> you can do?

    _____

Sentence Completions   Complete each sentence using a word from the box.

application	confident	current	experience	impression
opportunity	positive	previous	promoted	reliable

1. Tom handed his completed _____ to the interviewer.

2. Holly told the interviewer about her _____ job as a waitress.

3. Jose told the interviewer he wanted an _____ to work for the company.

4. Jan's _____ job, the one she had last year, was as a worker in a sales office.

5. Kevin wanted to be _____ to a better job in the same company.

Word Building   The word *review* has the prefix *re-* at the beginning. A **prefix** is a group of letters at the beginning of a word that changes the word's meaning. The prefix *re-* means "again." So, the word *review* means "to view again." Here is a sentence from the article:

Review what you have to offer.

That means you want to view again, or think again about what you have to offer an employer.

Add the prefix re- to the following words. Write the new words on the lines. Then define each new word. The first one is done for you.

1. try: _retry – to try again_

2. do: _____

3. play: _____

4. start: _____

5. marry: _____

TIP: Not all words that begin with re- are words with a prefix. You need to look at the word to decide if re- is a prefix. For example, in the words *relish* and *regular,* the re- is not a prefix.

Writing Activity   Write a short paragraph that correctly uses key vocabulary words to give some tips for doing well in an interview. Use at least four of the words from the list on page 15. Reread the definitions, if necessary.

_____

_____

_____

_____

_____

_____

_____

Think about your reading.

Check your comprehension.   Answer each question. If you don't know the answer, reread the lines in parentheses.

1. How can you prepare for an interview? (lines 8–12)

   _____

2. How should you dress for a job interview? (lines 31–32)

   _____

3. How can you make a good first impression in a job interview? (lines 53–55)

   _____

4. What should you do after a job interview? (lines 73–74)

   _____

Use reading skills: Identify main idea and details.

The **main idea** is what a reading is about. **Supporting details** tell about each main idea.

There is usually one main idea for a reading as a whole. Then each section within the reading has its own main idea. Every paragraph within a section will have its main idea, too. Main ideas at lower levels become the details for higher levels. For instance, section headings may identify details when you look at a reading as a whole. But each heading may also identify the main idea of its section. In the same way, the main idea of a paragraph may identify one detail within its section.

Identify main idea and details.   You can tell the main idea of this reading by its title. You know you will be reading about a job interview.

Look at the section headings in the article. Those will often tell you the supporting details for the article as a whole. On the lines below, list what you think are the main ideas of the different sections of the article.

_____

_____

_____

_____

Use a graphic organizer.

The center oval below shows the heading/main idea for the third section of the article. In each connected oval, write an important detail about that main idea.

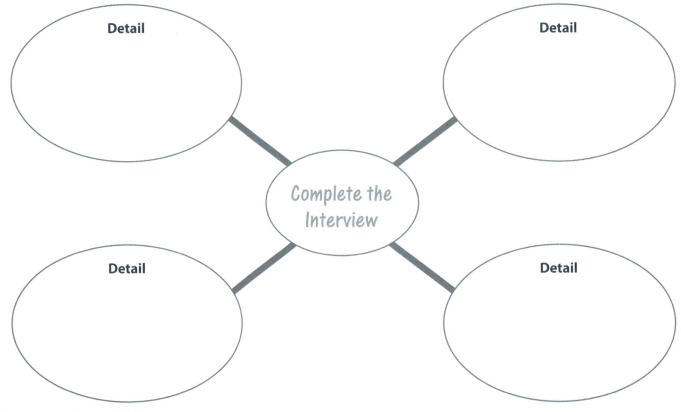

Write About It

Write a thank-you letter.

Start by thinking of a job you would like. Imagine you just had an interview for that job at a company you hope to work for. Write a thank-you letter to the person who interviewed you.

Prewriting   Thinking about main idea and details will help you when you plan your letter. Look at the graphic organizer below. Think of the main idea you want to tell the person who interviewed you. Write that in the center oval. Then write the details that back up your main idea. You may need more or fewer details. If you have more details, just draw another oval for each one.

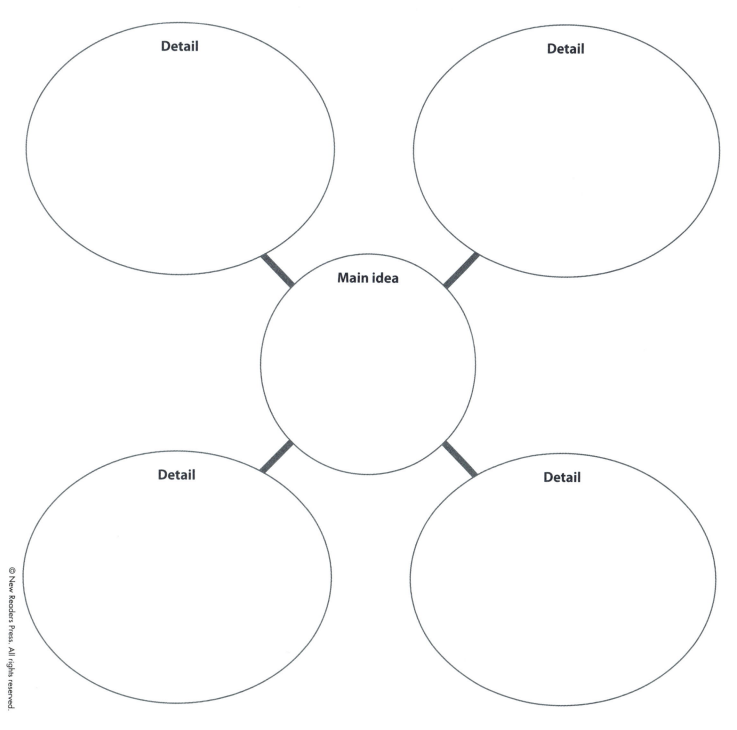

Thinking Beyond Reading Compare the graphic organizer you developed with a partner's graphic organizer. Each of you can talk about why you wrote what you did. If you get good new ideas, add them to your graphic organizer. Think again why you are writing:

- to thank the person for talking with you about the job

- to tell why you would be a good person for the job

- to make sure the person knows you want the job

Write a draft. On a separate piece of paper, write a first draft of your thank-you letter to the person who interviewed you. Follow standard business letter form, writing the heading, the body of the letter, and the closing as they appear here.

Your name
Your address

Date

Interviewer's name
Business address

Dear _____ :

Body of letter

Sincerely,
Your signature
Your name

Revise and create a final draft. Write your final draft on a separate piece of paper. As you revise, check your draft for these specific points:

- Did you write a topic sentence that sums up the main point of the letter?

- Did you include details to support your main idea?

- Did you follow standard business letter format?

- Did you check spelling and grammar to make sure your writing is clear and correct?

The Stepfamily

Learning Objectives

In this lesson you will:

▪ Read a story about family members trying to get along with each other.

▪ Learn to compare and contrast.

▪ Master the key vocabulary used in the story.

▪ Write an e-mail about a family's problem and how the problem was resolved.

Key Vocabulary

defiantly *(adverb)* showing willingness to fight or resist

dejectedly *(adverb)* in an unhappy way

determined *(adjective)* having a strong desire to do something even when it is difficult

exasperation *(noun)* the state of being deeply annoyed or irritated

hesitantly *(adverb)* slowly and uncertainly

ignore *(verb)* to pay no attention to

prompted *(verb)* encouraged someone to do something

reconciliation *(noun)* a situation in which people come back together after fighting

triumph *(noun)* victory

wearily *(adverb)* in a tired way

Before You Read

In this story you will read about a blended family. Begin by asking yourself these active reading questions: What is this story about? Who is blending in?

Predict what will happen.

1. Will the father get involved in the argument?

   _____

   _____

   _____

   _____

2. Will the girl stay as angry as she is?

   _____

   _____

   _____

   _____

Ask yourself questions.

1. How would I feel about having a stepmother?

   _____

   _____

   _____

   _____

2. What have I done to feel better when I've been as angry as the girl in the story?

   _____

   _____

   _____

   _____

Blending In

Read the story to find out what the problems are between Gilly and her stepmother. Highlight words and phrases that show how each of the characters feels.

"I hate you!" Gilly glared at her stepmother Doris and slammed the door.
Gilly's dad Franco heard the door slam. "What's that about?"
Doris sighed. "I asked her to clean her room. Again. Have you seen it?
There are piles of stuff. It's like a bomb went off in there."

5   Franco shrugged and turned back to the TV. "No big deal," he said.
Doris looked at him in **exasperation.** "She lives like a pig."
"I heard that," Gilly screamed through her door. Franco hunched down in
his chair and put his hands up over his ears.
Gilly sat on her bed, steaming. She picked up her cell phone and called

10   her best friend. "I really do hate her," she hissed into the phone, her teeth
clenched together. "Who does she think she is, my mother? I'm going to get
her. She is going to be gone. Out of here. She has no right. None."
The next day, Doris kept quiet. Gilly kept her room a mess. In fact she was
clearly making sure it looked worse. Once, she was leaving the bathroom and

15   **defiantly** glared at Doris as she dropped her wet towel on the bathroom floor.
"Pick that up!" Doris said sharply.
"You can't make me!" Gilly said. "Just try!" She turned her back and
slammed the door to her room again.
"Then you're grounded!" Doris yelled through the door.

20   Franco walked in the front door from work in time to hear the shouting
between his wife and daughter. "Now what?" he asked **wearily.** Doris told him,
spitting out her words.

"Don't make any plans this weekend. You're grounded," Franco said to Gilly through the door. "I've had it with you."

25   Gilly flung herself on her bed, sobbing and punching the pillow. *They'll be sorry. She is so gone. I hate her. I hate her. I hate her.*

1. Why do you think Gilly is unhappy?

    _____

2. How are Gilly, Doris, and Franco related to each other?

    _____

Gilly says she wants Doris *gone.* Keep reading to find out her plan. Mark the sentence when you first realize what Gilly's plan is.

     The next day, Gilly's stiff movements and silence showed how angry she still was. Doris tried at first to be forgiving, but after Gilly refused to respond to Doris's efforts at **reconciliation,** Doris got angry herself. "I'm here to stay," she

30 hissed at Gilly. "So get used to it."

     Gilly turned her back to Doris and didn't speak. *Here to stay. Get used to it.* The next day, Gilly went to her dad while he was fixing dinner. Doris was still at work. "Daddy?" she said **hesitantly.** Her father, happy to see she was speaking in a pleasant voice, smiled at her.

35   "Uh huh?"

     "There's something—well, it's kind of hard to say," Gilly said.

     Franco turned to Gilly and kept chopping. "What is it?"

     "Well," Gilly said, looking down at her hands, "I saw Doris at that restaurant Angelo's the other day."

40   "So?" Franco **prompted.**

     "Well," Gilly said, still looking down, "she was with some guy. They were talking, laughing, and holding hands. I didn't want to tell you, but I don't want you to get hurt."

     Franco stopped chopping. "Gilly, are you sure about this? I mean, really sure?"

45   Gilly, still looking down, nodded. Doris chose that time to come in the front door. "Look at these strawberries I got!" she said cheerfully to Gilly and Franco, **determined** to make things better. Franco stared at her, his arms hanging limply at his sides. Gilly kept looking down. Neither Franco nor Doris could see it, but a tiny smile of **triumph** moved over Gilly's lips.

3. What do you think Franco feels when Doris arrives home from work?

    _____

    _____

How will Franco respond to what Gilly said? Read on to find out if the family will solve its problems.

50   Gilly could hear them from the other room. "How could you?" her father was asking.

"But I didn't," Doris was saying, pleading. "I never did. I was at work then. I couldn't have. And I never would!"

"Are you saying Gilly would lie about something like this?"

55   Doris was silent for a minute. Then she said, with defeat in her voice, "You can think what you want. I didn't do anything. Franco, I'm not sure I can do this anymore. Gilly is willing to do anything she can to break us up, and I think she's winning."

Franco stared at her. Then he said, "I think we need help. We need
60 someone to help us figure out how to live together. Otherwise you're right. This will never work."

Doris shook her head. "I'm not sure," she said.

"No, wait, Doris," Franco said. "I know there are therapists who can help. Let me ask around and see if I can find someone."

65   Doris sat **dejectedly,** her head down. She shrugged.

The first session with the therapist was rough. Gilly said nasty things about Doris. Doris shouted back. Franco just sat with his head in his hands.

"You all need to cool off," the therapist, a woman named Beth, said. "You're not the first family to go through this, and you won't be the last. These
70 are tough relationships. But we can figure out ways for you to treat each other so you can live together and maybe even learn to like each other."

The therapist laid some ground rules. Doris wouldn't act as a parent. Only Franco could do that. But Franco had to pay attention and be a better father. He had to tell Gilly to pick up and not **ignore** the mess. In exchange, Doris
75 had to be friendly to Gilly and treat her as an aunt or a friend would.

They met with the therapist every other week. Franco knew they were going to make it one day when Gilly asked Doris to go shopping with her. He smiled cautiously to himself. He hoped that his family was going to blend after all.

therapists (noun)
professional people trained to help or treat people with problems

session (noun)
a meeting

4. If you were Franco, would you be smiling at the end of the story? Why or why not?

_____

_____

5. In your experience, are families usually as successful in improving their relationships as Gilly, Franco, and Doris were in this story? Discuss your ideas with a partner.

_____

_____

After You Read

Build a robust vocabulary.

Writing Sentences   Write a complete sentence to respond to each of the following questions or statements. Use the underlined word in your answer. Use the definitions on page 25 to help you.

1. Tell about a time when you spoke <u>defiantly</u>.

   _____

2. Tell about a time when you feel <u>exasperation</u>.

   _____

3. Has anyone ever <u>ignored</u> you when you were talking? What happened?

   _____

4. How do you feel when you do something <u>wearily</u>?

   _____

5. When do people speak <u>hesitantly</u>?

   _____

Sentence Completions   Complete each sentence using a word from the box.

defiantly	dejectedly	determined	exasperation	hesitantly
ignore	prompted	reconciliation	triumph	wearily

1. Mateo and I were friends again after our _____.

2. What _____ Gilly to make up a lie?

3. Gilly was angry. She spoke _____.

4. He knocked on the door again because he was _____ to get in and talk to me.

5. Doris wasn't sure, so she answered _____.

Word Building   A **suffix** is a group of letters added to the end of a word. When a suffix is added, a new word with a new meaning is formed.

The suffix -*ly* means "in a like way." Therefore, the word *sharply* means "in a sharp way." The word *wearily* means in "a weary way." Look at the following sentence from the story.

> Doris sat dejectedly, her head down.

You can tell by the suffix –*ly* that Doris was sitting in a dejected way.

Add the suffix -ly to the following words. Write the new words on the lines. Then define each new word and use it in a sentence. The first one is done for you.

1. joyful: _joyfully, in a joyful way_

   The baby clapped her hands joyfully when she saw the puppy.

2. prompt: _____

   _____

3. fond: _____

   _____

4. eager: _____

   _____

5. calm: _____

   _____

TIP: Words that end in *y* change the *y* to *i* when you add –*ly*. For example, *happy* becomes *happily* and *easy* becomes *easily*.

Writing Activity   Write a short paragraph that correctly uses key vocabulary words to tell what happens in the story. Use at least four words from the list on page 25. Reread the definitions, if necessary.

_____

_____

_____

Think about your reading.

Check your comprehension.   Answer each question. If you don't know the answer, reread the lines in parentheses.

1. Why does Doris get angry at Gilly? (lines 3–4)

   _____

2. Why does Gilly tell her father Doris was with another man? (lines 57–58)

   _____

3. What ground rule does the therapist say Doris has to follow with Gilly? (lines 72–75)

   _____

4. How does Franco know the family is getting along better? (lines 76–77)

   _____

Use reading skills: Compare and contrast.

When you **compare** things, you describe how they are alike. When you **contrast** things, you describe how they are different. For example, people might describe twins by saying that both children have blond hair and blue eyes, are the same height, and have the same smile. This is comparing. But although the twins may look alike, each may have different interests. One twin may like jogging while the other may like playing tennis. This is contrasting.

Compare and contrast. Can you compare and contrast Doris and Gilly from the story? Fill in the graphic organizer below. Write what is the same about Gilly and Doris in the space where the ovals intersect. Write what is different about them in the separate areas of each oval.

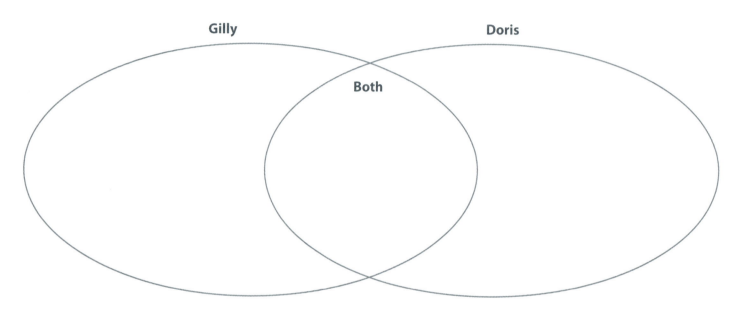

Gilly   Doris

Both

Use a graphic organizer.

You can compare and contrast how things or people change from the beginning to the end of a story. Fill out the table below to compare the family's relationships at the beginning of the story and at the end of the story.

Relationships at the Beginning of the Story	Relationships at the End of the Story

Write About It

Write an e-mail.

Every family has problems at one time or another. Write an e-mail to a friend that tells about a problem in your family or in a friend's family. Write about what caused the problem and what happened. Then write how the problem was resolved or the reasons why it was not resolved.

Prewriting Use this table to list your thoughts about the family's problem. You don't have to write complete sentences. You can write phrases that help you remember what you want to write about.

The problem

What caused the problem?

Has the problem been resolved? If yes, how?

Thinking Beyond Reading   Explain to a partner the problem the family was having. Talk about how things changed. Your partner may have some new thoughts you can add to your table. Add those ideas as you talk.

Write a draft.   Write a first draft of your e-mail. Use the ideas you listed in your table to guide you. Explain what the problem was. Tell who in the family was involved in the problem. Tell if things changed and if the problem was resolved. You may want to explore how the problem made the family members feel and how the family felt when the problem was resolved.

_____

_____

_____

_____

_____

_____

_____

_____

_____

_____

_____

_____

_____

_____

Revise and create a final draft.   Write your final draft on a separate piece of paper. As you revise, check your draft for these specific points:

- Did you tell how things were and how things changed?

- Did you write the events in the correct order?

- Did you check spelling and grammar to make sure your writing is clear and correct?

Living in a Community

Learning Objectives

In this lesson you will:

▪ Read a story about people who changed their community.

▪ Learn to identify cause and effect.

▪ Master the key vocabulary used in the story.

▪ Write a personal narrative about something you did that you were proud of and that helped someone out.

Key Vocabulary

discouraging *(adjective)* almost hopeless

dismay *(noun)* loss of courage, sudden disappointment

doubt *(noun)* uncertainty, loss of confidence

enthusiastic *(adjective)* with great interest

forceful *(adjective)* filled with great strength or energy

frowned *(verb)* made a facial look of displeasure

fuming *(verb)* feeling great anger

irritation *(noun)* a feeling of annoyance or bother

overwhelmed *(adjective)* overcome or helpless

vacant *(adjective)* empty

Before You Read

As you read the story, keep predicting what will happen next and checking your predictions. You can also summarize briefly what has happened in each section of the story. These active reading strategies can help you understand as you read.

Make predictions.

THINK ABOUT IT

1. Read the story title. What do you think the story will be about?

   _____

   _____

   _____

   _____

Something Good could be about many things. When I look at the picture, though, I can see that the story could be about cleaning up a messy lot.

2. What kinds of changes might take place after Jamal realizes that he just escaped a dangerous event?

THINK ABOUT IT

   _____

   _____

   _____

   _____

If I saw a bunch of guys try to hit me with a glass bottle, I might want to start a fight with them. But I know that nothing good ever comes from such a fight, and someone might get hurt. If Jamal is smart, he'll go home and work off his anger another way. I'll have to come back to this to see if that's what happens.

Summarize.

After you read a section of the story, try summarizing what happened in that section. In a few of your own words, tell what happened.

_____

_____

_____

_____

_____

_____

_____

_____

Something Good

Read the story to find out why Jamal is angry. Highlight or mark phrases that give clues about how Jamal is feeling.

What made Jamal mad was the bottle whistling by his head. He was walking by the **vacant** lot and noticed that someone had dumped another broken-down sofa there. "Junk," Jamal muttered to himself. "Nothing but junk." The sofa joined a stained mattress, a tangle of broken chairs, and heaps
5   of garbage in the lot. He saw the kids who were standing around smoking. They **frowned** when they saw him look at them. One picked up another bottle and aimed it at Jamal as if to threaten him.

Jamal was still **fuming** when he got to his sister's for dinner. "Place is a disgrace," he said to her. "It's like no one's got any pride around here." They
10   sat down to dinner. Jamal was still angry.

Finally, his sister said in **irritation,** "Well, change it, why don't you?"

Jamal snorted and pushed around the food on his plate with his fork. "You ever try to change anything around here?"

Jamal's sister put her hands on her hips and narrowed her eyes.
15   "Jamal Walker, that's lame. Who made you so weak? You want an idea? Here's an idea. Look at those red peppers you're eating. Know where they came from?"

Jamal shook his head and looked down at the vegetables. "They're from a community garden over in Tufts," Lakeesha said. "My friend Tonya works
20   there. She works; she gets some of what they grow. Why couldn't you do that? Or we could do it."

community (*noun*)
the people who
live in an area

Jamal stopped eating for a second. The idea sounded impossible. But if someone else had done it, maybe it wasn't. Trying not to show his interest, he said, "Right. You and me. We'll just start a garden."

25 Lakeesha hid her smile. She knew she had him. Then she shrugged, as if to show she wasn't that interested, either. "Probably a stupid idea anyway," she said. "Well, can't hurt to find out how they did it."

1. Why do you think Jamal is upset at the beginning of the story?

_____

_____

What do you think will happen next with the vacant lot? Keep reading to find out.

Lakeesha's friend was a very **enthusiastic** community gardener. Lakeesha found out all she wanted. "You talk to the owner of the land, get his OK to 30 clear it off and make the garden," Tonya said. "Seeds are cheap, and there's even a place where you can get them free, a community gardening group. You can get stuff called compost from them to put in the soil to make it richer, and you can borrow tools, too. I'm telling you, it's a great thing. And the stuff we grow—delicious."

35 Lakeesha sat back for a moment, **overwhelmed** with all she was hearing. Was she really up for this? Jamal chose that moment to walk in. He heard the last part of Tonya's breathless sentence. His reaction, though, was to get more interested, not less. "You really think we could do this?" he asked Tonya.

40 Tonya gave a **forceful** nod. "Oh, yeah," she said. "And I'm telling you, it'll be the best thing you ever did."

Lakeesha and Jamal went together to the company they knew owned the land. Getting their OK for the garden was surprisingly easy. The company had done a garden like that before, and there was even a water spigot on the 45 property they could use. They visited the community garden center. They got advice, seeds, compost, and tools to borrow.

Lakeesha and Jamal headed to the vacant lot. What a mess! Heaps of trash, broken furniture, rusty bedsprings. Jamal gave a sidelong look at Lakeesha and could tell from the look of **dismay** on her face that she was thinking 50 the same thing. She looked at him, her face full of **doubt.** Seeing her face made Jamal laugh. "Come on, Keesh," he said. "We're better than some nasty old bedsprings."

They got busy.

compost (noun)
  a mixture of soil and vegetable matter used to make soil richer

spigot (noun)
  a faucet or handle that controls water flow

2. What steps did Jamal and Lakeesha follow to create a community garden?

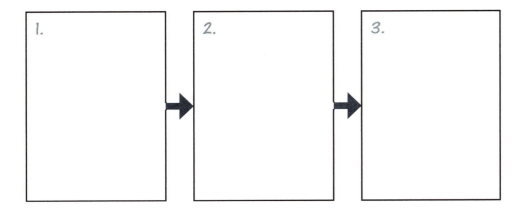

Finish reading the story to learn how the garden grows.

Later, both Lakeesha and Jamal would admit that without the other, they
would have quit. The work was hard and **discouraging.** There was so much
junk, and the soil was like rock. As they cleaned the lot up and dug into the
soil, neighbors came by. A few shook their heads, watching these fools wasting
their time in an ugly place. Some never looked their way. A few stepped into
the lot and began helping, hauling trash away and mixing compost into the
hard soil. Then they returned and brought others. The vacant lot became
a kind of low-key party. Someone made a sign: "The 145th Street Garden."
Someone else brought over a barbecue grill one day, and everyone brought
food to cook and share. They laughed and drank and ate. It felt good.

Lakeesha got a model garden design from the community garden people,
and marked off where to plant what. Vegetables, mainly, Lakeesha and Jamal
had decided. Flowers were pretty, but you couldn't eat them.

"I'm going to make a kind of schedule," Lakeesha announced to Jamal one
day. "Have people sign up to water and weed. That way we'll know who's here.
When those big old vegetables are ready, we can give them out to people who
helped."

That fall, there were peppers and cucumbers and squash and tomatoes.
People who took shifts would wander over to get a few tomatoes for dinner, and
there wasn't even much theft—too many people were around all the time. One
guy even made a bench. The garden was a cool, green place to be. "This is a fine
thing," Jamal said to Lakeesha one day as he sat on the bench with her. "We did
something. Not just us—all of us, I mean. We really did something good."

3. Why do you think Lakeesha set up a schedule?

_____

_____

After You Read

Build a robust vocabulary.

Writing Sentences   Write a complete sentence to respond to each of the following questions or statements. Use the underlined word in your answer. Use the definitions on page 35 to help you.

1. Why is Jamal <u>fuming</u> when he goes to his sister's house for dinner?

   _____

2. How do you know Tonya is an <u>enthusiastic</u> gardener?

   _____

3. Why does Lakeesha feel <u>overwhelmed</u> when she talks to Tonya?

   _____

4. When have you had <u>doubt</u> about the success of a project you were doing?

   _____

5. Tell about a <u>forceful</u> storm that you have experienced.

   _____

Sentence Completions   Complete each sentence using a word from the box.

discouraging	dismay	doubt	enthusiastic	forceful
frowned	fuming	irritation	overwhelmed	vacant

1. She knew Jamal was feeling _____ because he looked sad and gloomy.

2. The _____ lot needed a lot of work to become a community garden.

3. The boys _____ as they tossed the bottle at Jamal.

4. It was _____ to think about hauling away so much trash.

5. Lakeesha felt great _____ when her brother said that the garden was too big a project.

Word Building   Many different suffixes are used in the English language. Look at the chart below. It shows some common suffixes and their meanings.

Suffix	Meaning
–less	without
–ful	full of
–ness	state of being

Look at the words. Each one ends with a suffix. Draw a circle around each suffix.

| forceful | breathless | fullness |

Define each word. Use the meaning of the suffix to help you figure out what the word means. Then use the word in a sentence. The first one is done for you.

1. hopeful: *full of hope*

   He was hopeful that he passed the test.

2. stressful: _____

   _____

3. useless: _____

   _____

4. kindness: _____

   _____

TIP: You may have to change the spelling at the end of a word to add a suffix. For example, when you write the word *craziness,* you change the *y* in *crazy* to *i* and add –*ness.*

Writing Activity   Write a short paragraph that correctly uses key vocabulary words to summarize what happened in this story. Use at least four of the words from the list on page 35. Reread the definitions, if necessary.

_____

_____

_____

_____

Think about your reading.

Check your comprehension.   Answer each question. If you don't know the answer, reread the lines in parentheses.

1. How does Tonya feel about community gardens? (lines 33–34)

   _____

2. Where do Lakeesha and Jamal get the approval for the garden? (lines 42–43)

   _____

3. Who else helps out with the garden? (lines 56–60)

   _____

Use reading skills: Identify cause and effect.

The **cause** explains why something happens. The **effect** is what happens as a result of a cause. For example, if a big rainstorm floods the streets, the cause is the storm. The effect is the flood in the streets.

Identify cause and effect.   There is a cause and effect in the first part of the story. The cause is someone throwing a bottle at Jamal's head. The effect is that Jamal gets angry.

Reread the section of the story about the red peppers Lakeesha is serving:

"They're from a community garden over in Tufts," Lakeesha said. "My friend Tonya works there. She works; she gets some of what they grow."

1. Identify a cause in this section.

    _____

2. Identify an effect of the cause.

    _____

Use a graphic organizer.

Certain events in this story *caused* other results or *effects* to happen. Look closely at the information within the boxes below. Fill in the empty boxes to show the missing causes and effects.

Cause		Effect
Jamal gets angry about the vacant lot.	→	Jamal and his sister create a community garden.

Cause		Effect
Lakeesha and Jamal go to the community garden center.	→	1.

Cause		Effect
2.	→	They get vegetables from the garden in the fall.

Write About It

Write a personal narrative.

Think of a time when you did something that you were proud of that helped someone out. You might have helped a friend, or your family, or someone who just needed a hand. Think of what you did. Now think of the steps you took to help.

Prewriting Write the steps you took in the chart below. Each step was a cause that had an effect. List the causes and effects in the graphic organizer below. This will help you organize your thinking and your writing. Add more boxes if you need them.

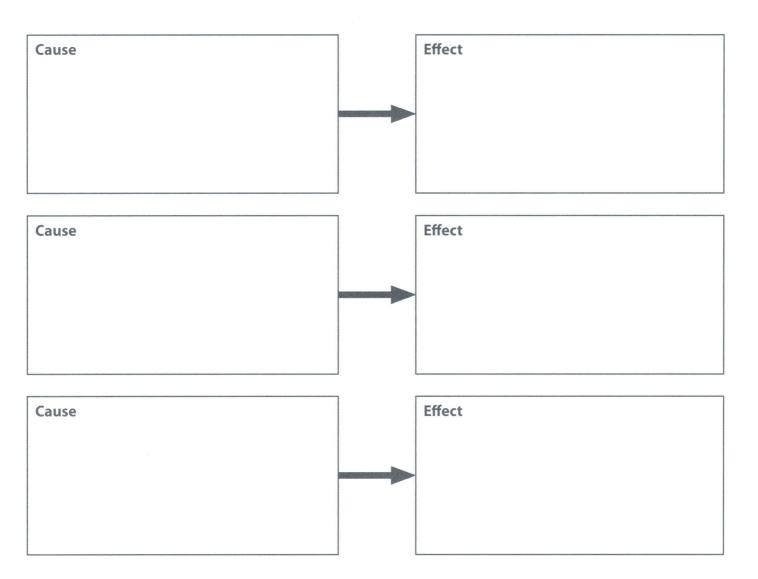

Cause	Effect
Cause	**Effect**
Cause	**Effect**

Thinking Beyond Reading   Explain to a partner the steps you took and the effect of each step. Have him or her ask questions about what you did. Then do the same for your partner. Add ideas to your graphic organizer to help make your personal narrative clearer.

Here are some possible questions to ask your partner:

- What were the most important steps you took?

- What was the effect of each of these steps?

- Overall, what was the result of your actions?

Write a draft.   Write a first draft paragraph that tells what caused you to feel proud of what you did. First, explain what you decided to do. Then write your paragraph, following the outline you wrote in the graphic organizer. Finally, write how you felt about helping and what the results of your actions were.

_____

_____

_____

_____

_____

_____

_____

_____

_____

_____

_____

_____

Revise and create a final draft.   Write your final draft on a separate piece of paper. As you revise, check your draft for these specific points:

- Did you start by explaining what you did and why?

- Did you write what happened in order?

- Did you tell the effect of each of the steps in your plan?

Learn a Trade

Learning Objectives

In this lesson you will:

▓ Learn about trade schools.

▓ Learn to make inferences from what you read and what you know.

▓ Master the key vocabulary used in the article.

▓ Write a summary of the article about choosing a trade school.

Key Vocabulary

administrative *(adjective)* having to do with management duties

available *(adjective)* able to be used

connections *(noun)* things or people that link together

enroll *(verb)* to join a school

license *(noun)* legal permission to do something

professions *(noun)* jobs that need special training

related *(adjective)* having to do with

reputation *(noun)* what people think about a person or organization

specific *(adjective)* certain

tuition *(noun)* payment to go to school

Before You Read

In this article, you will read about trade schools. Be an active reader. Decide what you want to learn from reading the article. Ask yourself questions as you read. Then try to find the answers.

Set a purpose for reading.

THINK ABOUT IT

Based on the title and the headings, I think this article will be about the types of schools that advertise on TV. I'd like to know more about them.

1. Have you ever been interested in learning a trade? Why or why not?

_____

_____

_____

2. What would you like to learn about trade schools?

_____

_____

_____

3. How can you use the information in this article to determine whether or not you'd like to go to a trade school?

_____

_____

_____

Ask yourself questions.

THINK ABOUT IT

I wonder if I could really get a job doing something else if I went to one of these schools. I'll read the article to find out.

1. Will I find out if trade schools are worth going to?

_____

_____

_____

2. Will this article convince me that I can get a better job if I go to a trade school?

_____

_____

_____

Is Vocational School Right for Me?

Read to find out how ads for vocational schools attract students. Mark phrases that tell what works in these ads.

You have probably seen the ads on TV. The smiling woman says, "Just a few short weeks with DIT, and you can have a great career!" Behind her you see pictures of happy students and other people chatting as they work in offices.

Can you really have a great career with a degree from a trade school
5 advertised on TV? The answer is—maybe. Going to vocational, or trade, school can be a smart move. Colleges offer a general education, but trade schools train people for **specific** careers. In most cases, you can complete vocational school in less time than it takes to get a college degree.

Some people, however, have found that the money they spent on a school
10 advertised on TV bought them nothing. There are good schools out there. The trick is to do your homework and find out which schools are worth your money and time.

Most of the trade schools you see advertised on TV are for-profit schools. They want you as a student because that's how they make money. And some of
15 these schools are worth the cost. They prepare students for **professions** such as truck driver, hair stylist, and **administrative** assistant.

Not all trade schools do a good job, though. Some promise more than they can deliver. You can spend plenty of money and time, and at the end be left with nothing. For example, schools may say there are jobs where few or no jobs
20 exist. They may say the pay for a job is much better than it is. The schools may not have the **connections** with businesses that they say they do. The teachers may not have the training they need to teach. The school may not have the equipment to train its students properly.

degree *(noun)*
a title given by a university or college to people who have completed a course of study

vocational *(adjective)*
having to do with a job or career

for-profit *(adjective)*
set up to make money

1. What is a for-profit school?

_____

_____

2. What are some jobs you can get by going to trade school?

_____

_____

It is wise to learn as much as you can about a school before you decide to enroll. Keep on reading to find out how to tell if a school is worth the money. Mark phrases that give this information.

Checking Out Schools

25   Before you sign up for school, do your homework. You can learn some trades on the job. You may not need to go to school at all. If you think that might be true of a job you want, check by calling an employer. Look for other ways to train other than going to a for-profit school. A community school or college may have the courses you need at a lower cost.

30   If you decide that trade school is a good idea, don't **enroll** at the first school you find. Find other schools that offer the training you want. Compare them to see which one offers the best training for the best price. Look closely at the schools you might go to. First find out how much each costs. Make sure you know what the **tuition** covers. Will you need to spend much more for books? Then find out how

35   many students find jobs when they graduate. How many drop out? Find out if you need a **license** to do the job. If so, how many of the students pass the licensing test?

Visit schools where you are thinking of enrolling. Do the students seem interested? How many students are in the classes? Talk to the students. Find out if they are happy with the school. Look at the equipment. Make sure it is

40   in good shape and is like the equipment you might use on the job.

Before you make a final decision, take one last step. Check out the school's **reputation** among employers. Do they hire the graduates of the school? Are the graduates ready to do the job when they finish school? In most states, schools need licenses to do business. Check with the state to find out if the school is accredited

45   and in good standing. That is, find out if the state thinks the school is doing its job. Check the school's ratings. You can also check with the Better Business Bureau to see if any consumer complaints have been filed against the school.

3. Where, other than trade school, might you find the courses you need?

_____

_____

accredited *(adjective)*
having official approval as a place that provides an education

4. What are some questions to ask at a school you are thinking about going to?

_____

_____

5. Why should you check with the state before you sign up for a trade school?

_____

_____

You've decided that trade school makes sense for you. Read on to find out how to get the most from your experience.

You're Going to School

The school may give you a contract to sign. Read it carefully. Make sure
50 the contract says what you were told when you decided to go there.

You will probably need some kind of financial help to attend school. The government has programs that offer aid through loans and grants . The school may have financial aid **available,** too. If you take out a loan, make sure you know how much you have to pay each month, what the interest rate is, and how
55 much time you have to pay the loan back. Then make sure you keep up with your payments. If you fall behind, you may have trouble getting other loans.

While you are taking classes, see if you can find work in a **related** field. Ask the school to help you find a job. You may get a job that is not your dream job. But remember, that job may help you get the job you want when you graduate.

60 Trade school is like any other school. If you don't go to class, you won't do well. The classes you take will help you prepare for the job you want. Some of the schoolwork will be bookwork, but it will help you do your job. Some of the schoolwork is likely to be hands-on training.

When you finish your studies, make sure to use the help the school offers.
65 They will have people who help their graduates get jobs. They may have lists of companies for you to get in touch with. Some schools have companies that come to them looking for people to hire.

When you graduate, you should be prepared to get the job you want. If that's the case, all your work will be worthwhile.

grants *(noun)*
awards of money
to pay for school

6. What are two places to look for help to pay for school?

_____

_____

_____

_____

After You Read

Build a robust vocabulary.

Writing Sentences Write a complete sentence to respond to each of the following questions or statements. Use the underlined word in your answer. Use the definitions on page 45 to help you.

1. Do you have a <u>license</u>? What kind?

   _____

2. Name two popular <u>professions</u>.

   _____

3. What does a person in an <u>administrative</u> job do?

   _____

4. What is a <u>specific</u> career you're interested in?

   _____

5. Name a job that is <u>related</u> to health care.

   _____

Sentence Completions Complete each sentence using a word from the box.

administrative	available	connections	enroll	license
professions	related	reputation	specific	tuition

1. I paid the _____ so I could go to school.

2. That trade school has a good _____ for getting its students jobs.

3. There are several jobs _____ at that company.

4. Did you _____ in school yet?

5. The school has good _____ with that company, so many students get jobs there.

Word Building If you want to compare two things, you usually add *–er* to the root word, for example, *long* becomes *longer* and *short* becomes *shorter*. With words that end in *y*, you change the *y* to *i* when you add *–er*. For example, *happy* becomes *happier* and *easy* becomes *easier*.

Read these words. Circle the ending that shows that the word is comparing two things.

straighter	higher	curlier	lower

Add an ending to each word below so that it becomes a word that compares. Use each word in a sentence that compares two things. The first one is done for you.

1. sharp: _sharper_

   The red pencil is sharper than the blue one.

2. pretty: _____

   _____

3. heavy: _____

   _____

4. dark: _____

   _____

Writing Activity   Write a short paragraph that correctly uses key vocabulary words to tell if you would like to go to a trade school. Use at least four of the words from the list on page 45. Reread the definitions, if necessary.

_____

_____

_____

Think about your reading.

Check your comprehension.   Answer each question. If you don't know the answer, reread the lines in parentheses.

1. How are trade schools different from colleges? (6–8)

   _____

2. What do you know about trade schools that don't live up to their promises? (lines 19–23)

   _____

3. What does it mean if a school is accredited? (lines 44–46)

   _____

4. What kind of schoolwork should you expect to do at a trade school? (lines 61–63)

   _____

Use reading skills: Make inferences.

You **make inferences** when you read. For example, if you read "He looked outside and put his raincoat on," you make the inference that it is raining outside. When you make an inference, you add what you read to what you already know.

Make inferences.   Read these sentences from the article. Write the inference you can make from each. The first one is done for you.

1.   Look closely at the schools you might go to.

   Inference: _Not all schools are equally good._

2.   Then find out how many of the students find jobs when they graduate.

   Inference: _____

3.   You can also check with the Better Business Bureau to see if any consumer complaints have been filed against the school.

   Inference: _____

Use a graphic organizer.

You can use a graphic organizer like the ones below to help you make inferences. Complete these two graphic organizers to make inferences.

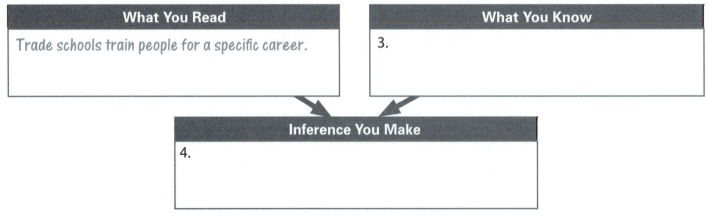

What You Read	What You Know
Compare different trade schools.	1.

Inference You Make

2.

What You Read	What You Know
Trade schools train people for a specific career.	3.

Inference You Make

4.

Write About It

Write a summary.

Knowing how to write a summary is a useful skill. You may need to remind yourself of the most important points in a chapter of a textbook, or your boss may want to know the most important points in a report. When you write a summary, you write the most important points. You leave out most of the details.

Prewriting Fill out the graphic organizer below with the most important points of the article you just read. You don't have to write complete sentences. A few words to remind you are enough.

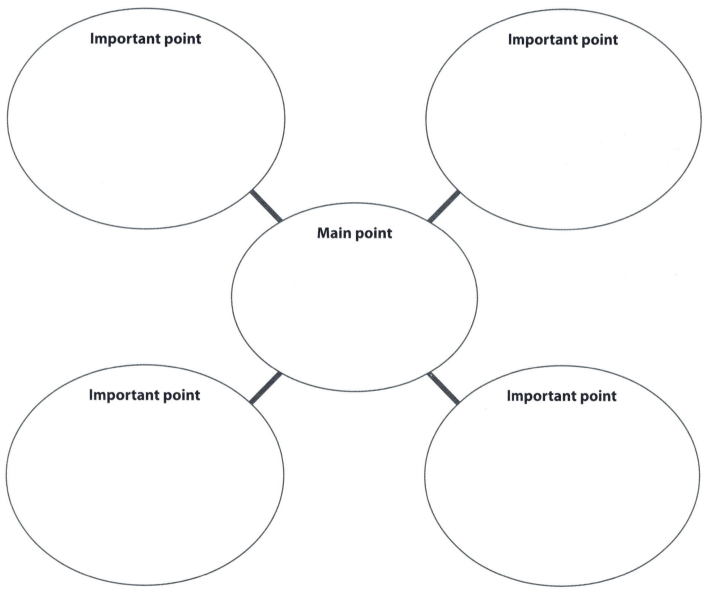

Thinking Beyond Reading   Discuss your graphic organizer with a partner. Add ideas to the graphic organizer as you talk. You may wish to think about these questions:

- What is the best way to choose a trade school?

- What ways are there to pay for school?

- Why are some trade schools better than others?

Write a draft.   Write a first draft of your summary paragraph. Begin with the main point of the article. Your topic sentence might be something like this: "Making a choice about a vocational school involves doing a lot of homework." Then add the important points from your graphic organizer. You may need more than one sentence to explain each important point.

_____

_____

_____

_____

_____

_____

_____

_____

_____

_____

_____

_____

_____

_____

Revise and create a final draft.   Write your final draft on a separate piece of paper. As you revise, check your draft for these specific points:

- Did you write a topic sentence that sums up the main point of the paragraph?

- Did you include the important points that support the main point?

- Did you check spelling and grammar to make sure your writing is clear and correct?

Trial by Jury

Learning Objectives

In this lesson you will:

▦ Read a story about a person who serves on a jury.

▦ Learn to synthesize, or put together, ideas.

▦ Master the key vocabulary used in the story.

▦ Write a paragraph that explains how the jury reached its verdict.

Key Vocabulary

attorney *(noun)* a person whose job is to give legal advice and to speak for people in court, a lawyer

innocent *(adjective)* not guilty

jealous *(adjective)* afraid of losing someone's love or attention to another person

reasonable *(adjective)* fair, sensible

testify *(verb)* to make a statement about what one knows

testimony *(noun)* evidence that a person swears is true

thoroughly *(adverb)* completely

unanimous *(adjective)* with everyone agreeing

viciously *(adverb)* violently or fiercely

witness *(noun)* one who saw what happened and tells about it

Before You Read

When you glance at the title of the lesson, you know it will have something to do with a trial. Begin by asking yourself an active reading question: What do I already know about trials and juries? Then, as you are reading, if you don't understand something, read it again to see if you get more meaning.

Use what you know.

THINK ABOUT IT

1. What do you already know about juries from TV shows? Do you think that knowledge is correct? What makes you think so?

   _____

   _____

   _____

   _____

   _____

My cousin was on a jury. The trial lasted a week. I know he was deciding a case about someone who was supposed to be a drug dealer. I think he got a lot of evidence to consider when hearing the case.

2. What do you know about juries and trials from experiences you or your family or friends have had?

   _____

   _____

   _____

   _____

   _____

   _____

Reread what you don't understand.

THINK ABOUT IT

When you don't know what a word or phrase means, reread the sentence or paragraph. The words and sentences surrounding the word you don't know may help you understand it. Try this with *jury summons* in the first paragraph. See if you can figure out what it means without looking at the definition.

I'm still not sure what a jury summons is. I'll reread the paragraph to see if I can figure out the meaning.

The Verdict

Read the story to find out how a jury reaches a verdict in a trial. Highlight the steps in the process. See if you agree with the jury's decision.

The envelope looked official. *Jury Summons* was written on the outside. Kaycee sighed. He didn't have time for this. He opened the letter and found he had to report to the court May 23 to possibly serve on a jury.

Kaycee's boss shrugged when Kaycee showed it to him. "You gotta do it," he
5   said. "And I gotta pay you, at least for the first three days. After that, I think the state pays you."

When Kaycee showed up at the courtroom on May 23 at 8:30 in the morning, the room was filled with people who looked as if they wanted to be somewhere else. First, they all watched a video about what to expect if they
10 were selected for a jury. Then the woman in front began calling numbers. Kaycee looked on his summons. 5223. A few minutes later, he heard his number and got up to join a group of people in a courtroom.

"This is a criminal trial," the court clerk announced. After a series of questions such as, "Have you ever been the victim of a violent crime?" people
15 were excused from the group. To his surprise, Kaycee found he was still in the room—and then on the jury.

The people who sat down in the jury box looked sideways at each other. The judge warned them. "Don't talk to anyone about the case. Don't read newspapers about the case. Don't go to places that have to do with the case."
20 The lawyers introduced themselves and began their opening statements. "This is a fairly simple case," the lawyer for the prosecution said. "Kevin Macon killed her because he was **jealous** and violent. We will prove beyond a **reasonable** doubt that he **viciously** stabbed his girlfriend Janice, killing her."

jury summons *(noun)*
  a notice to serve
  on a jury

prosecution *(noun)*
  people who represent
  the state and the victim
  against a person on trial

defense *(noun)*
    people who represent
    someone accused of
    committing a crime

The lawyer for the defense was equally firm in her statement. "The
prosecution is right. It is a simple case," she told Kaycee and the other jurors.
"But it is simple because Kevin Macon did not kill his girlfriend Janice. He loved
her. Janice was killed because of jealousy, but not Kevin's. We will prove that an
old boyfriend of Janice's killed her. Kevin is **innocent.** He is the victim here."

1. Have you ever gotten a jury summons? How did you feel about it?

   _____

2. What do you predict will be the conflict in this story?

   _____

So Kaycee is on the jury. Keep reading to find out what happens in the trial.

By now, Kaycee was **thoroughly** confused. During the prosecution's
opening, he was sure the guy was guilty. After the defense's statement, he was
equally sure the guy was innocent. "I guess that's why they have a trial," he
thought. "But I sure don't want to have to figure this out."

The prosecution began presenting its case. It told of the fights Kevin and
Janice had, and of shouting overheard on the day she died. "So what are you
going to do, kill me?" Janice had said. The prosecution told of Kevin's angry
response, although no one had heard the words he said. And it looked like
Kevin was the last one to see Janice alive.

"I don't know if he killed her, but he sure shouted at her that day," said an
older woman who lived next door. She sat on the **witness** stand clutching her
purse. "He was always doing that. I don't know why they stayed together. He
hit her, too. I saw the purple marks."

Then the defense lawyer asked the witness questions. "Where were you
when you heard this shouting?"

"Inside my apartment."

"So you don't know if someone else might have come to Janice's apartment
after the fight?"

"No. But—"

"Thank you," said the defense **attorney.**

Then the defense lawyer got up and had Kevin **testify.**

"We loved each other. I would never kill her. Sure, we had fights, but they
were all about this old boyfriend she kept seeing. She said she was scared of
him, so she kept seeing him. If you ask me, he did it."

The defense attorney had friends of Janice's testify about the mystery
boyfriend. "That was a creepy guy," one said. "None of us could stand him. Not
that Kevin was any better. He and Janice would get into some major shouting
matches, and once she showed me a cut she got when Kevin hit her."

3. At this point in the story, who do you believe and why?

_____

_____

What verdict do you think the jury will come to? Read on to see if you are right.

After four more days of **testimony,** Kaycee was itchy, tired, and ready to get back to work. At the end of that day, the attorney for the defense announced that her case was complete. After closing arguments, the jury got the case the
60 next day. As they filed into the jury room, Kaycee thought of all the movies he'd seen with juries trying to decide cases. It was just like that, he thought, twelve people in a little room trying to decide someone's fate.

Kaycee sat down with the others. Nice people, he thought. First, they elected a jury foreman . He was a teacher. Kaycee thought he seemed fair.
65 Then the hard work began. The foreman read the charge—second-degree murder. Then they began talking.

"He did it. Did you see the look on his face?" a young man with spiky hair said.

"We can't go on that," a serious young woman said. "If we have reasonable doubt about whether he did it, he's innocent. That's the law."
70 For a day and a half they went back and forth. The verdict had to be **unanimous.** Every time they took a vote, a few people—sometimes not the same people—voted innocent. After the sixth vote, the jurors sat looking at each other. Everyone was tired and getting cranky.

"Look," said the foreman, rubbing his forehead. "Let's go through this one
75 more time. The prosecution didn't give us the other boyfriend, the jealous one. All we have is some friends of hers talking about him. But Kevin was in the apartment. We know they were fighting. We know he could be violent. I think he did it, beyond a reasonable doubt. We really don't have any other suspects."

They talked again. They voted again. This time it was unanimous. Kevin
80 Macon was guilty. They filed back into the courtroom and the foreman read the verdict . Kaycee went home. He felt good about the verdict, he thought. It was the right one. That guy Kevin did it, didn't he? Kaycee shook his head. He had done the best he could. He just hoped they were right.

foreman (noun)
> a member of the jury who acts as its leader

verdict (noun)
> the decision of a jury about a case at trial

4. Why do you think the jury had trouble coming to a verdict?

_____

_____

5. Do you think the jury reached the right verdict? Why or why not?

_____

_____

After You Read

Build a robust vocabulary.

Writing Sentences   Write a complete sentence to respond to each of the following questions or statements. Use the underlined word in your answer. Use the definitions on page 55 to help you.

1. What is something an attorney does?

    _____

2. If you testify, what do you do?

    _____

3. What is a unanimous decision?

    _____

4. Tell about an animal that behaves viciously.

    _____

Sentence Completions   Complete each sentence using a word from the box.

attorney	innocent	jealous	reasonable	testify
testimony	thoroughly	unanimous	viciously	witness

1. When she gave her _____ in the case, she told the truth.

2. Jo read the book so _____ that she knew what was on every page.

3. I know he is _____ because I know he didn't do it.

4. The _____ told the jury she saw another woman leave with him.

Word Building   **Plurals** are words that mean *more than one.* If a person, place, or thing ends with *–s,* the *–s* often makes the word mean "more than one." Some people, places, or things change their spelling when the plural is formed. If a person, place, or thing ends with *x, s, ch, sh,* or *ss,* then you add *–es* to form the plural. For example *brush* becomes *brushes.* If a person, place, or thing ends with *y,* then you usually change *y* to *i* and add *–es.* For example, *puppy* becomes *puppies.*

Read this sentence from the story.

> Kaycee thought of all the movies he'd seen with juries trying to decide cases.

Three words in the sentence are plurals. They are *movies, juries,* and *cases.* Circle the root word in each of these words. Check your answers with a partner.

envelope	box	lawyer	injury

Look at the four words above. Can you add an ending to each one to make it a plural? Write the plural word below. Then use each one in a sentence. The first one is done for you.

1. envelope: *envelopes*

   The attorney showed the jury two envelopes.

2. box: _____

   _____

3. lawyer: _____

   _____

4. injury: _____

   _____

TIP: Not every word that ends in –s is a plural. Read nearby words to see if the word refers to more than one thing. For example, the word *kiss* ends in an *s* but is not a plural. *Kisses* is the plural form of *kiss*.

Writing Activity Write a short paragraph that correctly uses key vocabulary to tell about the case the jury is hearing. Use at least four of the words from the list on page 55. Reread the definitions, if necessary.

_____

_____

_____

Think about your reading.

Check your comprehension. Answer each question. If you don't know the answer, reread the lines in parentheses.

1. Why does the prosecution say Kevin Macon killed his girlfriend? (lines 21–22)

   _____

2. What does the witness who is the next-door neighbor say about Kevin Macon? (lines 38–41)

   _____

3. How did Kaycee feel about the jury foreman? (lines 63–64)

   _____

4. What was the verdict the jury reached? (lines 79–80)

Use reading skills: Synthesize information.

When you **synthesize,** you take parts of what you read and put them together to reach a new understanding. For example, if you read about how to walk, feed, and groom a dog, you could synthesize that information to explain how to take care of a dog.

Synthesize information.   Reread this section of the story to find the steps in the process of being chosen for a jury. Number the steps as you find them.

> The envelope looked official. *Jury Summons* was written on the outside. Kaycee sighed. He didn't have time for this. He opened the letter and found he had to report to the court May 23 to possibly serve on a jury.
>
> Kaycee's boss shrugged when Kaycee showed it to him. "You gotta do it," he said. "And I gotta pay you, at least for the first three days. After that, I think the state pays you."
>
> When Kaycee showed up at the courtroom on May 23 at 8:30 in the morning, the room was filled with people who looked as if they wanted to be somewhere else. First, they all watched a video about what to expect if they were selected for a jury. Then the woman in front began calling numbers. Kaycee looked on his summons. 5223. A few minutes later, he heard his number and got up to join a group of people in a courtroom.
>
> "This is a criminal trial," the court clerk announced. After a series of questions such as, "Have you ever been the victim of a violent crime?" people were excused from the group. To his surprise, Kaycee found he was still in the room—and then on the jury.

Use a graphic organizer.

You can use a graphic organizer like the one below to help you synthesize information. In the boxes, write the details that tell about being chosen, what a jury does during the testimony, and what happens in the jury room. You may need more or fewer boxes. Some are filled in for you.

How a jury works
1. people are chosen from jury pool
2. the court sends out jury summons
3.
4.
5.
6.

Write one or two sentences that synthesize the steps in being chosen for a jury.

_____

_____

Write About It

Write an explanation.

Explanations tell why something happened a certain way. Here, you will write to explain why the jury reached a guilty verdict in the trial of Kevin Macon. Think of what jury members learned during the trial. What points did they consider when coming to their decision? Use the graphic organizer below to list some of the factors that went into the jury's decision. Then use the information to support your explanation of why the jury reached its verdict.

Prewriting Complete this graphic organizer to show the points the jury considered in making its decision. Some of the ovals already have information filled in. You will use the information in this organizer to help you write.

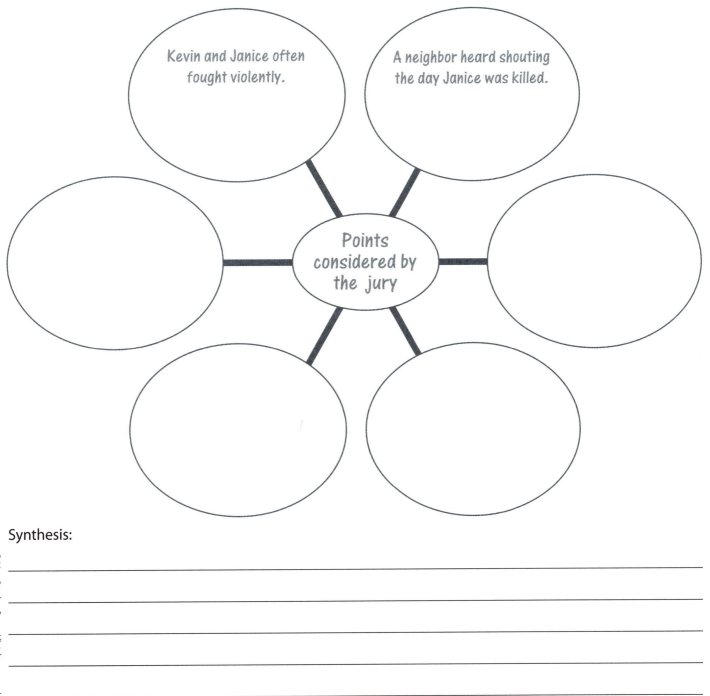

Synthesis:

_____

_____

_____

_____

Thinking Beyond Reading Think about these questions and discuss them with a partner. Add ideas to your graphic organizer as you talk.

- What evidence seemed to show innocence?

- What evidence seemed to show guilt?

- What other information did the jury use to decide its verdict?

Write a draft. Write a first draft of your explanation. First tell what you plan to explain. Use your synthesis to write a topic sentence such as this one: "The jury carefully considered all the evidence in order to reach a verdict." Then add the factors the jury considered as you write an explanation of why it came to its verdict.

_____

_____

_____

_____

_____

_____

_____

_____

_____

_____

_____

_____

_____

_____

_____

Revise and create a final draft. Write your final draft on a separate piece of paper. As you revise, check your draft for these specific points:

- Did you write a topic sentence that sums up what the paragraph is about?

- Did you write a clear explanation of the points the jury considered to reach its verdict?

- Did you check spelling and grammar to make sure your writing is clear and correct?

Staying Fit

Learning Objectives

In this lesson you will:

■ Learn about the benefits of walking.

■ Learn to make inferences.

■ Master the key vocabulary used in the article.

■ Write a description of a good fitness walk.

Key Vocabulary

combat *(verb)* to fight

companions *(noun)* people or pets you spend a lot of time with

disabled *(adjective)* unable to do certain things because of a physical or mental condition

effective *(adjective)* producing the result that is wanted

especially *(adverb)* to a great degree

evidence *(noun)* facts that show something is true

exertion *(noun)* an effort

gradually *(adverb)* slowly and evenly

incorporate *(verb)* to make a part of

processing *(verb)* the act of changing

Before You Read

As you begin to read this article, you will see that it is about the benefits of walking. Set a purpose for your reading, and ask yourself an active reading question: What are some of the benefits of walking? Also, think about how you feel when you take a walk. This helps you relate to the topic.

Make predictions.

THINK ABOUT IT

1. What do you think the article will tell you about walking and physical health?

   _____

   _____

   _____

   _____

There must be more to learn about walking than I thought. I bet I'll learn about different ways to walk that will help keep me fit.

2. What do you think the article might say about walking and mental health?

   _____

   _____

   _____

   _____

Make personal connections with the topic.

THINK ABOUT IT

1. How does taking a walk make you feel?

   _____

   _____

   _____

   _____

I have a friend who walks an hour every day. She's in great shape. Maybe walking can help keep me healthy.

2. Do you think walking might help you stay healthy? Why or why not?

   _____

   _____

   _____

   _____

Walk On

Read the article to learn about the health benefits of walking. Mark the sentences that give information about those benefits.

One of the simplest things to do is also one of the best for your health. All you have to do is walk. Unless you are **disabled,** you probably walk every day. That simple activity can keep you healthy if you do it right.

Walking can help your heart. People who walk can lower their risk of
5 having a heart attack. They can even lower their blood pressure. Walking can help with diabetes , too. Diabetes is a disease that keeps your body from **processing** sugar correctly. If you have diabetes, regular walking can help your body lower your blood sugar level. And since walking helps your body process sugar better, it can help you avoid getting diabetes in the first place.

10 A regular walking program can also help you keep your weight down. When you walk, you burn calories . Studies show that people who walk more than 10,000 steps every day have lower levels of body fat than people who don't walk that much. If you weigh 150 pounds and walk at a quick pace, you can burn 183 calories in a half hour. That may not sound like a lot. But if you
15 walk that much every day, you can make a long-term difference in your weight.

There is **evidence** that walking helps your mental health, too. If you suffer from depression , walking can help. Just changing the scene and getting outdoors might help lift the depression. But more importantly, walking releases chemicals in the brain that make you feel happier. So if you are stressed or
20 depressed, walking might help you feel better.

Walking can also help keep your bones healthy. If you start a regular program of walking now, you will probably have fewer problems with your bones as you get older.

diabetes *(noun)*
  a disease in which the body cannot properly control the amount of sugar in the blood

calories *(noun)*
  units of energy in food

depression *(noun)*
  a sad feeling that can last a long time

1. How can walking help a person with diabetes?

_____

_____

2. How can walking help keep your weight down?

_____

_____

Read on to find out how to get the most out of walking.

How to Walk

25   Walking might seem like the easiest thing in the world. In many ways, it is. That's part of what makes walking such an **effective** exercise for many people. All you have to do is step outside and get going. There are ways to make walking a better exercise, though. Make sure you have good shoes. They should be comfortable and have non-slip soles. Wear shoes that won't cause blisters
30 and will support your feet. Wear layers of clothing. Then if you get warm, you can take off a layer. When you walk at night, wear light-colored clothes and walk in well-lit places. That will help keep you safe.

    If you are new to the sport of walking, take it easy at first. Start off slowly. Plan to walk for about 20 to 30 minutes. Walk for 10 or 15 minutes and then
35 turn around and come back. As you keep walking, you'll be able to go farther and farther.

    Before you start walking, stretch. Warming up before you walk, **especially** if you will be walking quickly, reduces your risk of injury. Touch your toes. Raise your arms as high as you can above your head. Bend a leg and take your ankle
40 in your hand. Stretch out the muscles in your leg. Walk slowly for about five minutes to warm up your muscles. When you finish walking, do a cool down. Walk slowly and repeat the stretches you did to warm up.

    How fast should you walk? That depends on you. One easy way to tell if you are walking too fast is the "talk test." If you are walking and you can't carry
45 on a conversation, you are probably walking too fast.

3. What should you look for when you get walking shoes?

_____

_____

4. Why should you stretch before you walk?

_____

_____

In the next section, find out how to stick with walking. Underline the suggestions you like so you can remember them.

Making Walking Part of Your Life

To make walking an effective way to get fit, you need to make it a regular part of your life. Try to do it at the same time each day. If your goal is to improve your health, you need to walk about five times a week for at least 30 minutes. Many people like to walk first thing in the morning. They find it clears their heads and makes them feel better about the rest of the day. Also, they know they have started the day on a good note.

You can keep a walking log. Every day write how long and how far you walked. You may notice that as you get stronger, you can increase both your time and distance. Also consider buying a pedometer . When you walk, a pedometer notes how many steps you have taken. You could wear the pedometer all day and see how many steps you take.

Even if you can't find 30 minutes a day to walk, you can **incorporate** walking into your life in new ways. Take the stairs instead of the elevator. Park your car farther away from your place of work and walk. Think before you jump in your car. Ask yourself, *Do I have to drive or can I walk?* If you walk, you'll save money on gas as well as get some exercise.

As you keep walking, you may find yourself getting bored. To **combat** that feeling, set goals for yourself. For example, walk five minutes more every day for a week. Stay at that level of **exertion** for a week and then **gradually** increase the length of your walks. You can also switch off by walking fast for five minutes and then walking more slowly for five minutes.

If you make walking fun, you are more likely to keep doing it. Walk with a friend. Walking with a friend can motivate you. Make a date to meet every day. If you know someone is waiting for you, you are more likely to walk. You can also make walking fun by choosing different locations to walk. Walk downtown one day and through a park the next. Dogs are great walking **companions,** too. If you don't have a dog, borrow one.

However you do it, make walking a regular part of your life. Your body will thank you.

pedometer *(noun)*
   a device that counts
   how many steps
   a person walks

5. What are some ways to make walking fun?

_____

_____

_____

_____

After You Read

Build a robust vocabulary.

Writing Sentences Write a complete sentence to respond to each of the following questions. Use the underlined words in your answers. Use the definitions on page 65 to help you.

1. What might a <u>disabled</u> person not be able to do?

    _____

2. What did you do recently that required <u>exertion</u>?

    _____

3. If you <u>incorporate</u> walking into your life, what might happen?

    _____

4. What is one way to <u>combat</u> feelings of sadness?

    _____

5. When you go out, who are your most frequent <u>companions</u>?

    _____

Sentence Completions Complete each sentence using a word from the box.

combat	companions	disabled	effective	especially
evidence	exertion	gradually	incorporate	processing

1. If your body has trouble _____ sugar, you may have diabetes.

2. He _____ began to walk more, adding five minutes each week.

3. An _____ way to get fit is to walk every day.

4. I _____ like to walk in the park because it is so pretty there.

5. There is _____ that walking every day can help keep you healthy.

Word Building In the word *friendly,* the word *friend* is the **root word** that other words are made from. You can add prefixes and/or suffixes to the root word *friend* to make these words:

friends	unfriendly	friendship	friendliness

Circle the root words in *walking* and *healthy.* Check your answers with a partner.

happiness	player	places	easiest

Look at the four words above. Can you find the root word in each of them? Write each root word below. Then write other words you can make from the root word by adding prefixes and/or suffixes. The first one is done for you.

1. colorful: _color – colors, colorless, coloring, recolor_ _____

2. happiness: _____

3. player: _____

4. places: _____

5. easiest: _____

TIP: If you don't know what a word means, look for a root word within it. That may help you figure out the meaning of the word.

Writing Activity   Write a short paragraph that correctly uses key vocabulary words to tell how walking can help keep you healthy. Use at least four of the words from the list on page 65. Reread the definitions, if necessary.

_____

_____

_____

_____

Think about your reading.

Check your comprehension.   Answer each question. If you don't know the answer, reread the lines in parentheses.

1. How can walking help with depression? (lines 17–19)

_____

2. What should you wear when you walk at night? (lines 31–32)

_____

3. How can you tell if you are walking too fast? (lines 44–45)

_____

4. What does a pedometer do? (lines 55–56)

_____

Use reading skills: Make inferences.

You **make inferences** all the time. When you read or learn something new and add the new ideas or information to what you already know, you make an inference. Inferences make reading a richer experience.

Make inferences.   You can make an inference about different kinds of walking. Reread this section of the article.

> One of the simplest things to do is also one of the best for your health. All you have to do is walk. Unless you are disabled, you probably walk every day. That simple activity can keep you healthy if you do it right.

You know from the paragraph that walking can keep you healthy. You know from your experience that many people walk, but they aren't that healthy. What inference can you make by putting together what you read and what you know?

_____

_____

Use a graphic organizer.

You can use graphic organizers to help you make inferences. Complete the graphic organizer below to make an inference.

What You Read	What You Know
You can burn 183 calories in a half hour by walking.	An average candy bar has 200 calories.

Inference You Make
1.

Read the sentence in the graphic organizer below. Then add what you know. Complete the graphic organizer to make an inference.

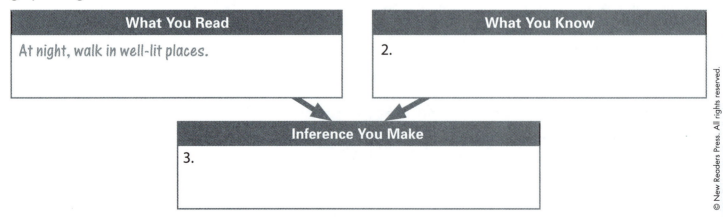

What You Read	What You Know
At night, walk in well-lit places.	2.

Inference You Make
3.

Write About It

Write a description.

A description gives details about something. Often a description will tell you how something feels, looks, sounds, or smells. Write a description of a fitness walk. Include details that tell the reader what it is like to take a fitness walk.

Prewriting   Fill out this graphic organizer with the details you want to include in your description. Write the details in the ovals around the main idea *What a fitness walk is like.* You may want to include details that tell what a person might see, hear, and smell on a fitness walk.

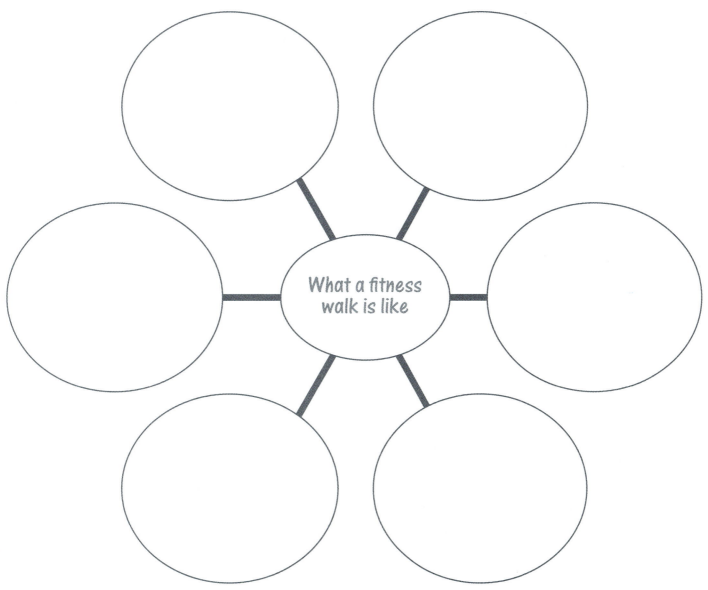

Thinking Beyond Reading   Discuss a fitness walk with a partner. You can ask each other these questions to see if there are additional details you want to add to your graphic organizer.

- What is the difference between a fitness walk and a stroll?

- What might you hear on a fitness walk around a park?

- What might you see?

- What might you smell?

Write a draft.   Write a first draft paragraph of your description. Your topic sentence might be something like this: "What you hear, see, and smell on a fitness walk is different from what you might experience when you walk from your car to your apartment." As you write, imagine someone reading your paragraph. See how real you can make the experience for the reader.

_____

_____

_____

_____

_____

_____

_____

_____

_____

_____

_____

_____

_____

_____

Revise and create a final draft.   Write your final draft on a separate piece of paper. As you revise, check your draft for these specific points:

- Did you write a topic sentence that tells what the paragraph is about?

- Did you include details that describe the experience?

- Did you check spelling and grammar to make sure your writing is clear and correct?

Owning a Home, Losing a Home

Learning Objectives

In this lesson you will:

■ Read a story about Joyce's problems and her mortgage payments.

■ Make judgments about the decisions made by the main character.

■ Master the key vocabulary used in the story.

■ Write a letter to the editor.

Key Vocabulary

despair *(noun)* the loss of all hope

eventually *(adverb)* at a much later time

expiration *(adjective)* the point at which something is no longer good, such as food

misery *(noun)* deep unhappiness

possessions *(noun)* things people own

proceedings *(noun)* legal actions

reassuring *(adjective)* restoring confidence

reduced *(adjective)* lowered

rickety *(adjective)* shaky, not sturdy

subdued *(adjective)* toned down

Before You Read

You know from the title that this story is about losing a home. Begin reading by asking yourself an active reading question: What do I want to get out of reading this story? Also, try to visualize, or make pictures in your mind of what is happening, as you read. This helps you relate to and remember what you are reading.

Set a purpose for reading.

THINK ABOUT IT

1. What do you think you might learn about housing in this story?

_____

_____

_____

_____

I want to buy a house, so I'll read to find out what I can learn from this story. I don't want to have any problems when I buy a house.

2. How could this story help you?

_____

_____

_____

_____

Visualize while you read.

THINK ABOUT IT

1. Picture in your mind the look on Joyce's face when she threw a letter from her mortgage company in the trash. Describe the look on her face.

_____

_____

_____

_____

I know the news in the letter is not good. Joyce probably looks scared and upset. I can picture the look on her face.

2. Contrast that look with the look on Joyce's face when she first bought the house. Describe the difference.

_____

_____

_____

_____

Losing a Home

Read this story to find out what happens when a homeowner has problems paying her home loan. Highlight or mark sentences that show the process Joyce goes through.

When Joyce saw the letter, she quickly crumpled it up and threw it in the trash. She didn't bother to open it. She knew the grim news inside. Another missed mortgage payment. Joyce put her head in her hands. What could she do? There wasn't even enough money to pay for food. Quietly, she began to sob
5   into her hands. **Despair** washed over her, and panic.

Joyce remembered when she signed the papers for the house. After years of saving, Joyce had enough for a small down payment.

"Congratulations," the gray-haired man in a suit had said. He shook her hand and smiled warmly. She hadn't been able to stop the grin spreading over
10   her face. It was a small house, but big enough for Joyce and her two children. That was one of the proudest days of Joyce's life.

For two years, Joyce had made the payment every month. Every month, she felt a small thrill as she wrote the check for the house. She was a homeowner. **Eventually,** she would own this house. Her job as a stocker in a store was good
15   and steady. Maybe not the best paying, but if she was careful, the pay was adequate. The kids were happy. They were doing well in school. Life was just fine.

Things started to fall apart when the accident happened. It was stupid, really, Joyce thought to herself. She should never have been on that **rickety** ladder in the first place. But then she'd fallen and hurt her back. She had to
20   go to the emergency room that night. They took x-rays. It was the beginning of the nightmare she was living now. Joyce didn't have health insurance. The hospital kept sending bills. She paid what she could, but the bills were huge.

mortgage (noun)
a loan on a house

down payment (noun)
part of the price of a house paid when a loan for the house is taken

More important, Joyce's injury meant she had to leave her job. Now there was no money coming in. Every time the phone rang, it was another creditor .

1. Should Joyce have bought the house? Use what you know to make a judgment.

_____

_____

The bills won't stop coming. What do you think Joyce should do next? Read on to see what she decides. Mark or highlight sentences that give hints about her thinking process.

25　　Joyce had a little money in savings, but that was quickly gone. Her parents gave her a little, but they weren't rich. Meanwhile, the bills kept coming. Joyce paid what she could, but she didn't have the money for everything. Lights and food were the most important, Joyce figured, so she paid for those. All the other bills piled up. She went two months without paying her mortgage.

30　　Then the letters began. In serious language, they warned that she was late with her payments—something Joyce knew better than they did. After a while, Joyce stopped opening the bills.

　　The kids knew something was up. They had walked in one day when she was sobbing at the kitchen table. Jade looked at her and patted her back. Now, 35　Joyce noticed, they seemed **subdued,** not laughing as much. They didn't ask for any money, either.

　　Joyce found a part-time job in a store, but she couldn't work more than that. Her back hurt too much. Joyce got creative with food. She cooked a lot of beans and rice. She bought meat that was **reduced** in price because it was 40　almost at its **expiration** date.

　　One day, Joyce's friend Maria was there when another bill from the mortgage company came. Joyce didn't even look at it. She just threw it in the trash.

　　"What are you doing?" Maria asked. "Are you throwing out bills now?"

　　"I can't pay it," Joyce said. "What's the point?"

45　　"Listen," Maria said. "You call the bank. Tell them what happened. Maybe they'll cut you some slack. They do that sometimes. You want to lose this house? Because that's the next thing that's going to happen. Foreclosure . Ever heard of it?"

　　"Course I heard of it," Joyce said. "But I don't have any money. I can't pay 50　what I don't have, so why should I talk to anyone?"

　　Maria just shook her head. "You gotta at least try," she said. "There are things they can do. Reset the mortgage. Maybe sell the house and pay off the mortgage. But they sure can't do any of that if you stick your head in the sand."

　　Joyce just shook her head in **misery.** "It's no use," she kept saying.

2. How would you feel if you were in Joyce's shoes?

_____

_____

People keep calling Joyce to collect their money. What can she do? Read on to find out. Underline the sentences that give hints about whether or not Joyce will be able to start over.

55   Finally, one day a man from the bank came over. "You haven't been paying your mortgage," he said.

"I know," Joyce said. "I got sick, I lost my job . . ."

"You should have come and talked to us. It's too late now," the man said. "We have to foreclose. You know what that means?"

60   "You take the house. I know that," Joyce said miserably.

"Afraid that's right," the man said. "We started foreclosure **proceedings.** You'll have to be out of here soon."

"You can't stop it? There's nothing I can do?"

"It's like I said," the man replied. "We probably could have done
65 something, but not now. The wheels are moving."

For about two months, nothing more happened except the phone calls and the bills. They never stopped. Then another man came to the door.

"Ma'am, the bank is taking over this house," he said. "You need to be out by Saturday. If you're not out, your **possessions** will be removed. I'm sorry," he
70 said, as Joyce's eyes filled with tears.

That week, Joyce did the one thing she hadn't wanted to do. She took a deep breath and called her parents. "Mom? It's Joyce," she said. "They're taking the house. Can the kids and I move in there?"

For a while, there was silence. Joyce could see her Mom shaking her head,
75 thinking about Joyce losing the house, about three more people in the little house Joyce grew up in. "Sure, honey," her mom said. "For a while. That's what family's for."

That Friday, Joyce borrowed a friend's truck and spent all day moving their stuff over to her parents' house. Jade and her brother Bo watched wide-eyed as
80 the truck drove away with all their things.

"Don't worry," Joyce whispered to them, giving them a **reassuring** hug. "It'll be fine. We'll start over. It'll be all right."

3. Was Joyce's decision to move herself and the kids back to her parents' house a good one? Use what you know to help you make a judgment.

_____

_____

After You Read

Build a robust vocabulary.

Writing Sentences   Write a complete sentence to respond to each of the following statements. Use the underlined word in your answer. Use the definitions on page 75 to help you.

1.   Tell about something you will <u>eventually</u> do.

_____

2.   Name some of your <u>possessions</u>.

_____

3.   Describe how you <u>reduced</u> your spending in the past.

_____

4.   Describe a <u>rickety</u> chair.

_____

5.   Tell about a time when you felt <u>despair</u>.

_____

Sentence Completions   Complete each sentence using a word from the box.

despair	**eventually**	**expiration**	**misery**	**possessions**
proceedings	**reassuring**	**reduced**	**rickety**	**subdued**

1.   You will feel great _____ if you are sitting in the cold rain without a hat.

2.   She looked at the _____ date on the box and saw the crackers were old.

3.   The _____ at court decided who should pay the bill.

4.   Marge found the quick hug _____.

5.   Hal had been whistling happily, but when he saw his grade, he became _____.

Word Building   Many different prefixes are used in the English language. Look at the chart below. It shows some common prefixes and their meanings.

Prefix	Meaning
pre–	before
post–	after
un–	not

Look at these words. Draw a circle around the prefix in each word.

| uncomfortable | prehistoric | postwar | unhappy |

Define each word below. Use the meaning of the prefix to help you figure out what the word means. Then use the word in a sentence. The first one is done for you.

1. uncomfortable: _not comfortable_

    She felt uncomfortable speaking in front of the class.

2. prehistoric: _____

    _____

3. postwar: _____

    _____

4. unhappy: _____

    _____

TIP: Use what you know about prefixes to figure out what an unknown word means. For example, knowing the prefix *un-* will help you understand that *unkind* means "not kind."

Writing Activity   Write a short paragraph that correctly uses key vocabulary words to tell what happened to Joyce. Use at least four of the words from the list on page 75. Reread the definitions, if necessary.

_____

_____

_____

_____

Think about your reading.

Check your comprehension.   Answer each question. If you don't know the answer, reread the lines in parentheses.

1. Why did Joyce have to leave her job? (lines 19–23)

    _____

2. Why did Joyce throw out the bills? (lines 43–44)

    _____

3. Why did the man at the bank tell Joyce that she must leave her house? (lines 61–62)

    _____

Use reading skills: Make judgments.

One part of being a good reader is **making judgments** about what you read. When you do this, you use what you know to consider issues in a story or article. You might decide if you agree with a course of action. You might also make a judgment about a character. For example, you might decide that a character is generous, selfish, kind, or lacks patience.

Make judgments.   In this story, Joyce makes some decisions. Reread this section of the story that tells about a decision she makes.

> Things started to fall apart when the accident happened. It was stupid, really, Joyce thought to herself. She should never have been on that rickety ladder in the first place. But then she'd fallen and hurt her back.

Joyce is thinking about a decision she made. What is your judgment of Joyce's decision to go up on the ladder? Discuss your judgment with a partner. Did you both judge her actions the same way? Or were your judgments different? Explain.

_____

_____

_____

Use a graphic organizer.

You can use a graphic organizer like the one below to help you make judgments. Fill in the chart with the judgments you make about Joyce's actions.

Joyce's actions	Your judgments. Tell why you feel this way.
Joyce won't open her bills.	1.
Joyce doesn't tell her children what is going on until the problem has become a crisis.	2.

Write About It

Write a letter to the editor.

A letter to the editor may be an opinion about something in the news. But sometimes, letters to the editor give information the writer thinks people should know. Imagine that Maria wants people to know what happened to her friend Joyce. She wants to warn people of the dangers of foreclosure. She wants to give people information about how they can avoid losing their houses.

Prewriting The main idea of the letter is to tell people about the dangers of foreclosure and how they can avoid it. Use this web to jot down the points you want to cover in your letter about foreclosure.

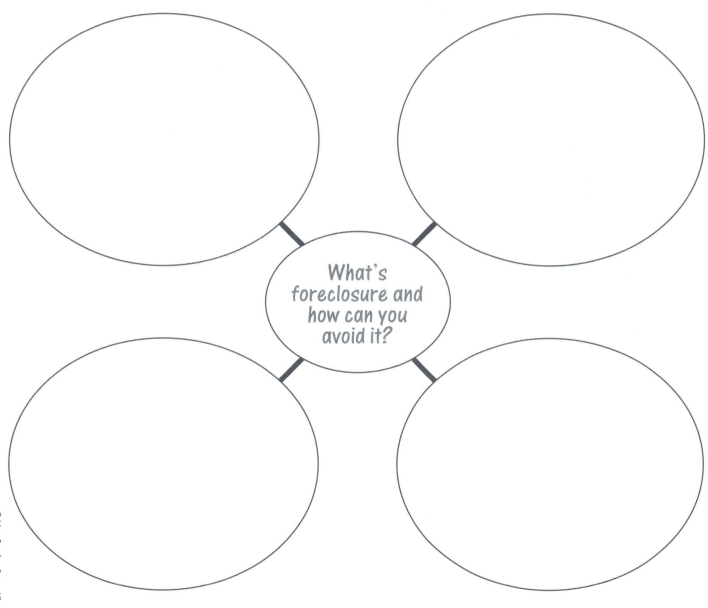

Thinking Beyond Reading Think about these questions and discuss them with a partner. Add ideas to the graphic organizer as you talk.

- What did you learn about foreclosure from reading the story?

- Why do you need to act if you want to avoid foreclosure?

- What can a person who is afraid of foreclosure do?

- What kind of effect might foreclosure have on other members of your family?

Write a draft. On a separate piece of paper, write a first draft of your letter to the editor. Follow the form of a business letter, writing the heading, the body of the letter, and the closing as they appear here.

Your letter might begin with this summary of the main point: "My friend just went through the terrible experience of losing her home to foreclosure. It didn't have to happen. Here's what you can do to make sure it never happens to you." As you write, try to imagine the person reading the letter. Use the details in your organizer to help you organize your ideas. Make your letter as clear and as specific as you can.

> Your name
> Your address
>
> Date
>
> Newspaper's name
> Newspaper's address
>
> Dear Editor:
>
> Body of letter
>
> Sincerely,
> Your signature
> Your name

Revise and create a final draft. Write your final draft on a separate piece of paper. As you revise, check your draft for these specific points:

- Did you tell what foreclosure is?

- Did you tell the reasons why a person's house might go into foreclosure?

- Did you list steps a person can take to avoid foreclosure?

- Did you follow standard business letter form?

- Did you check spelling and grammar to make sure your writing is clear and correct?

Healthy Eating

Learning Objectives

In this lesson you will:

▨ Learn about the fats in food.

▨ Learn to classify information.

▨ Master the key vocabulary used in the article.

▨ Write a description of how to lower the fat in a high-fat meal.

Key Vocabulary

dense *(adjective)* containing a lot of things that are very close together

excess *(adjective)* extra

ingredients *(noun)* foods that are used to make something

margarine *(noun)* a food similar to butter

methods *(noun)* ways of doing something

prepared *(adjective)* made ahead of time

reduce *(verb)* to lower

structures *(noun)* arrangements in definite patterns

substance *(noun)* a particular material

surface *(noun)* the outside of something

Before You Read

As you read, think about what you already know about the fats in food. Reread slowly anything you don't understand. See if that active reading strategy helps your understanding.

Use what you know.

1. What do you already know about the fats in the food you eat?

_____

_____

_____

_____

_____

I know there are fats in meat like bacon. Fat is the white, slick stuff in meat. I wonder if all fat looks like the fat we can see in meat.

2. What do you think you might learn from the article about fats?

_____

_____

_____

_____

_____

_____

Reread what you don't understand.

When you read a difficult section of the article, reread it. Rereading will help you better understand what you read.

I'm not sure I understand what polyunsaturated fats are. I'll read the paragraph again, this time more slowly, and see if that helps me figure out the meaning.

Know Your Fats

There is more to fats than butter and bacon. Read this article to find out about the fats in our diets. As you read, highlight the information about each type of fat.

Everyone knows that some foods have a lot of fat. When you eat a piece of bacon, you know that the greasy feel is fat. Some fat is hidden, though. You may not know, for example, that there is fat in a muffin. Knowing about the fat in your diet can help keep you healthy.

5 We all need some fat in our diets. Fat provides much of the energy we need. Most adults, though, get more fat than their bodies need. This **excess** fat can lead to weight gain. Some kinds of fat can lead to disease, so it is important to watch how much and what kind of fat you eat.

To choose the right kinds of fat, you first need to know more about fat

10 in general. Fats are made of building blocks called fatty acids. There are three kinds of fat: saturated , polyunsaturated , and monounsaturated fat. Their names describe the chemical **structures** of the fats.

Saturated fat is found mostly in animal fat. It's the white fat you see on beef. This kind of fat is also found in milk and cheese. Your liver uses

15 saturated fats to make cholesterol . Your body needs some cholesterol, but too much of this **substance** can cause heart disease. Cholesterol can build up in the arteries and slow blood flow. That can lead to a heart attack or stroke.

saturated fat (noun)
a fat found in dairy and meat products, also in some plant oils

polyunsaturated fat (noun)
a fat found in grains, fish, and seafood

monounsaturated fat (noun)
a fat found in plants like avocados, nuts, and olives

cholesterol (noun)
a substance in the body that can cause heart disease

1. Why do people need fat in their diets?

_____

_____

2. What are fatty acids?

_____

_____

Fats turn up in all kinds of unlikely places. Read on to find out where. Put arrows in the margins by the most important things you learn.

hydrogenated fat (noun)
   a liquid fat that has been hardened into a solid

trans fats (noun)
   fats produced when liquid vegetable oils are hydrogenated

20   Polyunsaturated fat is found in oils from grains like corn and soybeans. It is also found in fish like herring and salmon. Monounsaturated fats are also liquid. They include vegetable and nut oils such as peanut and olive oil. Both polyunsaturated and monounsaturated fats are better for you than animal fats. They are good to use in cooking. However, like all fats, they are high in calories.

25   Sometimes polyunsaturated and monounsaturated fats are hydrogenated . If a fat is hydrogenated, it has been changed from a liquid to a solid. For example, corn oil, which is a liquid, is hydrogenated to create stick **margarine,** which is a solid. Hydrogenating vegetable oils produces trans fats . Trans fats can be found in most margarines, most fried foods, and many commercial

30   baked goods. Doctors say trans fats are even worse for us than saturated fats, and should be avoided.

You know you need fat in your diet. But how can you make healthy choices in the amount and type of fat you consume? The first thing you can do is look at the amount of fat in your diet. Can you **reduce** the overall amount of fat you

35   eat? Fat in all its forms should account for less than 30 percent of the calories you eat. Remember that fat is **dense** in calories. A pat of butter has about the same number of calories as a small apple.

You can also be a fat detective. Fat is sneaky. It can turn healthy foods into unhealthy ones. For example, on its own, a chicken breast is fairly low in

40   fat. When it is fried, though, the number of calories nearly doubles. Being on the lookout for extra calories can help you reduce the overall amount of fat in your diet.

Check the labels on the foods you eat to find out the types and amounts of fat they contain. Nutrition labels on **prepared** foods tell you the number

45   of calories and the number of calories from fat in a serving. They also tell you how much saturated fat and trans fats are in the food. Let's say you are shopping for margarine. Not all margarines are the same. Compare the ingredients on the nutrition labels. Buy the one that is lowest in saturated and trans fats.

3. What percentage of the calories you eat should be from fat?

_____

_____

4. Where can you learn how much fat is in prepared food?

_____

_____

When you cook, you can take steps to use less fat. Read on to find out what those steps are. Number the steps in the text as you read them.

50   You can make a difference in the amount and type of fat you eat when you prepare food at home. Use **ingredients** that are low in fat. For example, you can make mashed potatoes with broth instead of butter. You can put low-fat or fat-free milk in your coffee. You can serve leaner cuts of meat. Look closely at the meat's **surface.** Avoid buying meat with lots of white streaks running
55   through it. The white streaks mean it has lots of saturated fat.

When you cook, choose cooking **methods** that use little or no fat. For instance, you can broil or bake chicken, fish, and meat instead of frying them.

You can also make healthier choices when you eat out. If you have a choice between a burger and fries or a chicken breast and salad, choose the chicken.
60   Ask the restaurant to grill your meat instead of cooking it in butter. And ask for the salad dressing on the side. That way, you decide how much you put on your lettuce.

By eating less of all the fats and by being aware of what kind of fat you are eating, you can make a big difference in how you feel and how healthy you are.

5. What steps can you take to reduce the amount of fat in your diet?

_____

_____

_____

_____

_____

After You Read

Build a robust vocabulary.

Writing Sentences   Write a complete sentence to respond to each of the following questions or statements. Use the underlined word in your answer. Use the definitions on page 85 to help you.

1. Tell about the effects of <u>excess</u> fat in the diet.

   _____

2. Do you use <u>margarine</u>? If so, how do you use it?

   _____

3. What are the <u>ingredients</u> in your favorite sandwich?

   _____

4. What <u>prepared</u> foods do you like to eat?

   _____

5. If you <u>reduce</u> the fat in your diet, what will probably happen?

   _____

Sentence Completions   Complete each sentence using a word from the box.

dense	excess	ingredients	margarine	methods
prepared	reduce	structures	substance	surface

1. The chemical _____ of fats are described in their names.

2. Fat is a _____ found in many foods.

3. There is a layer of fat on the _____ of the soup.

4. Grilling and broiling are healthy _____ for cooking meat and fish.

5. Fat is _____ in calories.

Word Building   There are many **prefixes** for quantity. *Uni-* means "one," *bi-* means "two," *tri-* means "three," and *multi-* means "many." Knowing the meanings of these common prefixes can help you figure out what a word means.

Look at the words below. Circle the prefix that shows a quantity.

multimedia	unicycle	bilingual	triangle

Define each word below. Use a dictionary if you need to. Then use the word in a sentence. The first one is done for you.

1. multimedia: _many kinds of media_

    That was a great multimedia presentation.

2. unicycle: _____

    _____

3. bilingual: _____

    _____

4. triangle: _____

    _____

TIP: Make sure the beginning of a word is a prefix and not part of the root word. For example, in the word *multiply, multi-* is not a prefix.

Writing Activity   Write a short paragraph that correctly uses key vocabulary words to tell how to reduce the fat in your diet. Use at least four of the words from the list on page 85. Reread the definitions, if necessary.

_____

_____

_____

Think about your reading.

Check your comprehension.   Answer each question. If you don't know the answer, reread the lines in parentheses.

1. In what kinds of food are you most likely to find saturated fat? (lines 13–14)

    _____

2. How can you tell how many fat calories there are in prepared foods? (lines 44–46)

    _____

3. How can you tell whether a margarine contains trans fats? (lines 47–48)

    _____

4. What are two ways to make eating at restaurants healthier? (lines 58–61)

    _____

Use reading skills: Classify information.

When you **classify,** you sort information. For example, you could classify which foods in this article contain unhealthy fats and which foods do not. Classifying helps you get more meaning from what you read.

Classify information. Reread this part of the article. It gives examples of two of the fats in our daily diet.

> Polyunsaturated fat is found in oils from grains like corn and soybeans. It is also found in fish like herring and salmon. Monounsaturated fats are also liquid. They include vegetable and nut oils such as peanut and olive oil. Both polyunsaturated and monounsaturated fats are better for you than animal fats. They are good to use in cooking. However, like all fats, they are high in calories.

You could classify the fats by whether they come from animals or plants. What other way could you classify them?

_____

_____

_____

_____

Use a graphic organizer.

You can use a graphic organizer like the one below to help you classify information. Fill in the organizer. Classify some of the foods in the article by the type of fat they contain. It may be helpful to review the article and the definition of each type of fat before you begin.

Examples of Types of Fat

Saturated Fat	Polyunsaturated Fat	Monounsaturated Fat
butter	corn oil	peanut oil

Write About It

Write a description.

When you write a description, you include specific details that help the reader form a picture in his or her mind. Write a description of a high-fat meal you have made. Then describe ways you could lower the fat. Write about the lower-fat ingredients you will use, and how you will prepare the foods to reduce fat.

Prewriting   A graphic organizer like the chart below can help you classify information. Fill in the chart to classify the ingredients and cooking methods in your meal. Use some of the suggestions from the article for ideas to lower the fat in your high-fat meal.

My Meal

Food	Ingredients and Cooking Methods	
	Higher Fat	**Lower Fat**

Thinking Beyond Reading   Discuss your high-fat and lower-fat meal with a partner. Review these questions to see if you want to add more information to your organizer.

- What are some ingredients you can change in your meal?

- What are some ways you can reduce the fat in your meal?

- Do you have any other suggestions to help your partner make his or her meal even lower in fat? Does your partner have any ideas for you?

Write a draft.   Write a first draft description of your high-fat meal and how you can lower the fat. You might begin your first paragraph like this: "My family often eats a high-fat meal of steak, mashed potatoes, green beans with butter, and ice cream. But there are ways to reduce the fat in our meal without losing any of the flavor." Use the details in your chart to describe ways you can lower the fat in each of the dishes of your meal.

_____

_____

_____

_____

_____

_____

_____

_____

_____

_____

_____

Revise and create a final draft.   Write your final draft on a separate piece of paper. As you revise, check your draft for these specific points:

- Did you write a strong topic sentence that sums up the main idea?

- Did you include details that describe the types of food, the ingredients, and how the food was prepared?

- Did you check spelling and grammar to make sure your writing is clear and correct?

Being Money Smart

Learning Objectives

In this lesson you will:

▪ Learn about payday loans.

▪ Determine if a statement is a fact or an opinion.

▪ Master the key vocabulary used in the article.

▪ Write an e-mail to a friend that warns about the dangers of payday loans.

Key Vocabulary

advance *(noun)* money given before it is earned

consumers *(noun)* people who buy goods and services

desperate *(adjective)* having no way to escape from or solve

employer *(noun)* one who hires people to do work

identification *(noun)* legal papers that tell who someone is

lure *(verb)* to attract into a trap

outrageous *(adjective)* beyond normal or acceptable limits

overdraw *(verb)* to take more money from an account than is in the account

predatory *(adjective)* taking advantage of others for personal gain or profit

thriving *(adjective)* doing very well, growing

Before You Read

Decide what you want to learn from reading this article about the money problems of a woman who got a payday loan. Be an active reader by asking yourself questions and trying to find the answers as you read.

Set a purpose for reading.

1. What would you like to learn from this article?

   _____

   _____

   _____

   _____

2. Would information about payday loans be helpful to you? Why or why not?

   _____

   _____

   _____

   _____

Ask yourself questions.

1. What are the problems with payday loans?

   _____

   _____

   _____

   _____

2. Why do people take out payday loans?

   _____

   _____

   _____

   _____

Payday Loans: Beware!

If you have ever been tempted by the "Get Money Now!" signs on payday loan stores, read on. Highlight or mark the facts that show how expensive these loans are.

June was in trouble. Payday was still a week away, and she had no money left from the last paycheck. None. She had to eat, so she did the only thing she could think of. She got a payday loan.

June decided she could survive if she had $100. She wrote a check to the payday loan company for $115. To June, it seemed like a good deal, $15 dollars in exchange for enough money to eat. The check was dated for her next payday, in a week. When payday came, she went back to the loan store. "You can roll it over," the clerk told her. She could pay a little more, and keep the money another two weeks. June thought of how tight money was. She agreed. By the time she had rolled over the loan three times, she had paid $60 in interest for her $100 loan. That's an interest rate of 60 percent for only seven weeks. In contrast, interest on a house loan is often 10 percent or less per year.

Sometimes these loans are called payday loans. Sometimes they are called check **advance** loans or cash advance loans. You have probably seen the ads on TV or seen the stores offering them. Often the ads are colorful and loud. "Need money NOW? Come in!" To someone who is feeling **desperate,** the ads may seem like an answer from heaven. But be very careful before you write a check to a payday loan company. These companies are **predatory.** These loans are some of the most expensive you can get. They are even illegal in some states.

There is one bright spot in the world of payday finance. Since the Truth in Lending Act passed, **consumers** must be told the cost of all loans. If you take out a payday loan, the lender must tell you, in writing, the dollar cost of

5

10

15

20

roll over *(verb)*
   to have a loan
   continued

interest *(noun)*
   money you pay to
   borrow money

finance charge *(noun)*
a charge for
borrowing money

the finance charge and the annual percentage rate of interest, or the APR. This is the cost of credit on a yearly basis.

1. Why does June keep rolling over her loan?

   _____

2. What is the Truth in Lending Act?

   _____

Read on to find out why payday loan companies are so popular, and why some are illegal.

25   To get a payday loan, all you need is a bank account and checks that can be written on that account. The payday loan company does not check your credit or check to see if you can repay the loan. If you have proof that you have a job, a checking account, and **identification,** you can get a payday loan.

       When your next payday comes, the payday loan company will cash the
30   check you wrote. But let's say you are still short when payday comes around and the payday loan company cashes the check. Now, you are looking at even more charges from both the bank and from the lender. A single bounced check can cost $40 or more in fees. In the worst cases, the bank may close the account. After that, the consumer may have trouble opening another bank
35   account. He or she may also have a negative credit rating . That would make it difficult to get other loans or credit cards.

credit rating *(noun)*
a rating that tells banks
and others how well a
person pays back loans

       Even though payday loan companies may seem like a bad group of businesses, they are **thriving.** There are about 25,000 payday loan stores in the United States. Together, they loan about $28 billion a year. Consumers pay
40   about $5 billion in fees for those loans each year.

       Payday loan companies may be greedy, but for some desperate consumers, they at least offer a solution to money problems. Other payday loan companies, though, are flat out illegal. Some are in states that do not allow such loans. In those states, small banks may let payday loan companies use the banks to offer what are really
45   payday loans. These loans, like payday loans, are extremely expensive.

       Some payday lenders try to **lure** customers with gifts and prizes. Before Christmas, when many people want to spend money on gifts for family, payday lenders pounce. Advertising for payday lenders goes up. Some offer free t-shirts or turkeys to lure the desperate.

3. How do payday lenders lure customers?

   _____

   _____

Read on to learn other ways to get money quickly. Highlight or underline the ideas you think are most important.

50   What can desperate people do, besides pay the **outrageous** fees of payday lenders? There are other, better ways to get money, even for the desperate. First, check around if you think you need a loan. Companies that offer loans may want your business. Check with your bank and with other banks and loan companies. Check with the place you work. Your **employer** may be willing to give you a
55   small loan until payday. If you have a credit card, you may be able to get a loan on the card. It will be expensive, but not as expensive as a payday loan. In a pinch, a close friend or family member may be able to help you out. Even if you have to pay some interest, almost any loan will be cheaper than a payday loan.

Another way to try to solve your financial problems in the short term
60   is to go directly to the people you owe money to. They may be credit card companies. Maybe you owe money to the electric or phone company. Call them up. Tell them what you are facing. They will at least know that you want to solve the problem. They may charge you a late fee or an extra finance charge, but that will still be cheaper than a payday loan.

65   Talk to your bank about overdraft protection . That is a loan your bank will give you if you **overdraw** your account. There is a finance charge for that, too. It is a loan, after all. Like these other solutions, though, overdraft protection is much cheaper than a payday loan.

The best way to avoid payday loans is to avoid needing them. Set up a
70   budget. Watch the everyday purchases that can quickly eat up your money before you notice. For example, a specialty coffee can cost $3.00 or more. If you buy one every work day for a month, that's at least $60.

There are non-profit groups that charge nothing to help people get their spending on track. They can teach you how to make and stick to a budget.
75   You can get control of your budget—and you will never have to think about a payday loan again.

overdraft protection (noun)
a loan your bank can give you automatically when you spend more than you have in your account

4. Do you know anyone who has ever gotten a payday loan? If so, tell what you know about how the money got paid back. Do you know if there were any issues?

_____

5. How might your employer help you avoid needing a payday loan?

_____

_____

6. What can you do to avoid needing any kind of expensive loan?

_____

_____

After You Read

Build a robust vocabulary.

Writing Sentences   Write a complete sentence to respond to each of the following questions or statements. Use the underlined word in your answer. Use the definitions on page 95 to help you.

1. Describe an <u>outrageous</u> statement someone could make.

   _____

2. What do <u>consumers</u> do?

   _____

3. If someone asked for your <u>identification</u>, what would you show him?

   _____

4. Why would someone ask for a cash <u>advance</u> loan?

   _____

Sentence Completions   Complete each sentence using a word from the box.

advance	consumers	desperate	employer	identification
lure	outrageous	overdraw	predatory	thriving

1. Some think payday loan companies are _____ because of how they treat customers.

2. If you _____ your bank account, people you wrote checks to may be angry.

3. Payday loan companies are _____ because so many people need money quickly.

4. Some _____ people keep renewing payday loans even though those loans are very expensive.

5. To get a payday loan, all you need is a job, a bank account, and some _____.

Word Building   Compound words are words made of two or more smaller words. You can often tell the meaning of a compound word by looking for the two smaller words. *Bookcase, fireplace, sunset,* and *haircut* are all compound words.

Read this sentence from the article.

> Like these other solutions, though, overdraft protection is much cheaper than a payday loan.

There are two compound words in the sentence. They are *overdraft* and *payday*. Circle the two smaller words in each of these words. Check your answers with a partner.

Read these compound words from the article. Each word is made up of two smaller words.

payday	paycheck	someone

Decide the meaning of each compound word by thinking about the meanings of the two smaller words. Write the meaning of each word on the line below. Then use each compound word in a sentence. The first one is done for you.

1. payday: _the day I get paid_____

   _On payday, I'll go to the grocery store._____

2. paycheck: _____

   _____

3. someone: _____

   _____

TIP: If you don't know a long word at first, see if it is a compound word. Is it made up of two smaller words? You may be able to figure out its meaning if you know what the two smaller words mean.

Writing Activity   Write a short paragraph that correctly uses key vocabulary words to tell what payday loans are. Use at least four of the words from the list on page 95. Reread the definitions, if necessary.

_____

_____

_____

Think about your reading.

Check your comprehension.   Answer each question. If you don't know the answer, reread the lines in parentheses.

1. What are other names for payday loans? (lines 13–14)

   _____

2. What do you need in order to get a payday loan? (lines 25–28)

   _____

3. Name three places to look for money other than payday loan companies. (lines 51–58)

   _____

4. How can you avoid needing a payday loan in the future? (lines 69–71)

   _____

Use reading skills: Identify fact and opinion.

Many articles are a mixture of fact and opinion. Being able to tell the difference helps you better understand what you read. **Facts** can be proven. For example, "Some states don't allow payday loans" is a fact. **Opinions** are the feelings or beliefs of the writer. "Payday loans are bad for consumers" is an opinion.

Identify fact and opinion.   As you began to read this article, you could tell that the writer had an opinion. The title is "Payday Loans: Beware!" That tells you from the start that the writer has an opinion about payday loans. She doesn't like them. Reread this part of the article about payday loans and think about what is fact and what is opinion.

> To someone who is feeling desperate, the ads may seem like an answer from heaven. But be very careful before you sign your name on a check to a payday loan company. These loans are some of the most expensive you can get. They are predatory. They are even illegal in some states.

Draw a single line under a fact in this passage. Draw a double line under an opinion. In other words, find a statement that can be proven to be true. Then find a statement that tells you what someone thinks or feels.

Use a graphic organizer.

You can use a graphic organizer like the one below to help you separate facts from opinions. Fill in the organizer by writing some facts and opinions about payday loans from the article.

Facts	Opinions
1.	4.
2.	5.
3.	6.

Write About It

Write an e-mail.

Your local lawmakers are thinking of passing a law banning payday loans in your town. The new law would make payday loans illegal and would close all of the payday loan stores in your area. Write an e-mail to your lawmaker stating your opinion on whether the new law should be passed. Back up your opinion with facts from the story.

Prewriting Use the graphic organizer below to help organize information for your e-mail. Fill in the center oval with your opinion for or against the new law. Then fill in the outer ovals with facts from the story that support your opinion. You can use this information when you write your e-mail.

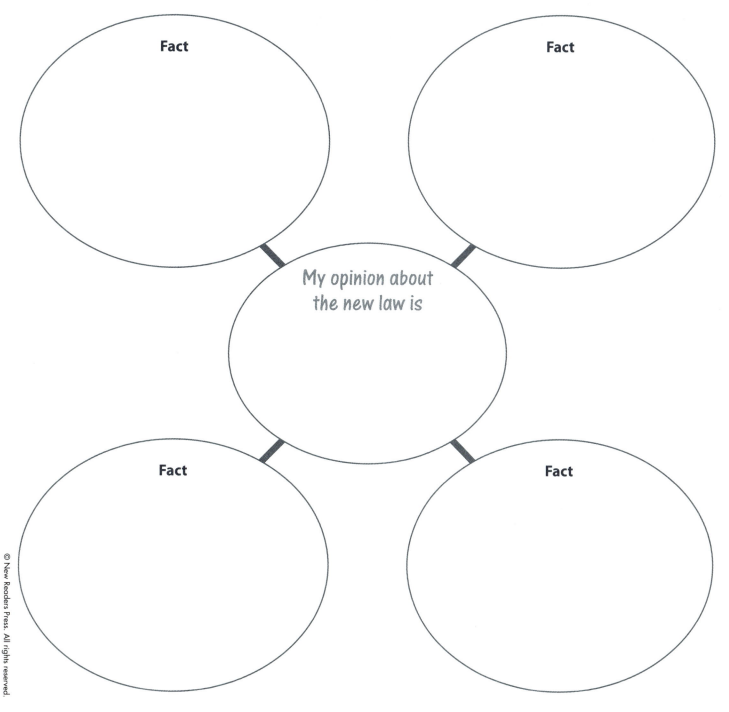

Thinking Beyond Reading   Discuss with a partner whether you think payday loans should be illegal. You can also discuss these questions and add additional information to your graphic organizer.

- Is there ever a good time to get a loan? Explain why or why not.

- What types of loans are fair to both the lender and the borrower?

- Is it ever worth paying a high interest rate on a loan in order to get out of financial difficulty? Why or why not?

- Do you think a loan can ever get a person out of financial difficulty? Why or why not?

Write a draft.   Write a first draft of your e-mail. Clearly state your opinion for or against passing the new law to make payday loans illegal. Be sure to include facts from the story to back up your opinion. Begin your e-mail with a greeting. Use the organizer you completed to help you add details to your argument. Add more lines if you need to.

_____

_____

_____

_____

_____

_____

_____

_____

_____

_____

_____

Revise and create a final draft.   Write your final draft on a separate piece of paper. As you revise, check your draft for these specific points:

- Did you clearly state whether or not you think the new law should be passed?

- Did you add enough facts from the story to back up your opinion?

- Did you include a greeting?

- Did you check spelling and grammar to make sure your writing is clear and accurate?

Answer Key

Lesson 1 Choosing Happiness
pp. 5–14

Writing Sentences
Sample answers:

1. In my <u>leisure</u> time, I like to go biking.

2. Two <u>habits</u> of mind that can make a person happy are forgiveness and feeling grateful.

3. Married people might have <u>conflicts</u> about money or how they spend time.

4. I have good <u>relationships</u> with my wife and my friends.

5. When I <u>concentrate</u>, I feel focused.

Sentence Completions

1. anxious

2. dwell on

3. Recognizing

4. Poverty

5. negative

Word Building
Circle *time, feel, happy.*

Sample answers:

2. watch: She likes watching basketball.

3. search: The researcher asked a lot of questions.

4. friend: That was an unfriendly dog.

5. forgive: He asked for her forgiveness the next day.

Writing Activity
Answers will vary. Review the vocabulary words and the definitions. Find the words in the article to see how they are used.

Check your comprehension.
Sample answers:

1. Watching TV isn't likely to make people happy because when they are watching TV, they aren't active.

2. Forgiving others can make you happy because you let go of negative thoughts.

3. A new car won't make you happy for long because you will get used to it and want something else.

Draw conclusions.
Sample answers:

1. Watching TV is not an active way to spend time. Being active makes people happy.

2. I watch TV about four hours a night to catch up on the news and to relax. I feel like I'm sitting around a little too much.

3. I could be happier if I watched less TV.

Use a graphic organizer.
Sample answer:

If I spend more time with my close friends, I will be happier.

Prewriting
Answers will vary but should include suggestions such as watching less TV, exercising more, forgiving, spending more time with family, or making new friends.

Thinking Beyond Reading
The graphic organizer might now include more suggestions for being happy.

Write a draft.
Answers will vary, but should include information from the idea web on page 13.

Revise and create a final draft.
The final draft should begin with a topic sentence that sums up the main point of the paragraph. It should have few grammatical and usage errors.

Lesson 2 Getting the Job
pp. 15–24

Writing Sentences
Sample answers:

1. My <u>experience</u> using the Internet helped me get a job.

2. Dressing well helps me to feel <u>positive</u> about an interview.

3. Looking the interviewer in the eye helps make a good <u>impression</u>.

4. Always arriving on time shows I'm <u>reliable</u>.

5. I'm <u>confident</u> I can make elderly residents comfortable.

Sentence Completions
1. application

2. current *or* previous

3. opportunity

4. previous

5. promoted

Word Building

2. redo: to do again

3. replay: to play again

4. restart: to start again

5. remarry: to marry again

Writing Activity

Answers will vary. Review the vocabulary words and the definitions. Find the words in the article to see how they are used.

Check your comprehension.

Sample answers:

1. To prepare for an interview you might find out about the company and then think about questions they might ask you.

2. For a job interview, dress nicely and make sure your clothes are neat and clean.

3. You can make a good first impression in a job interview by holding out your hand with a smile, looking the interviewer in the eye, and showing the interviewer you are excited about the job.

4. After a job interview, you should send a thank-you letter.

Identify main idea and details.

Sample answer:

The main ideas of the sections of the article are preparing questions and answers, planning for the interview, completing the actual interview, and thanking the interviewer.

Use a graphic organizer.

Sample answers:

Arrive early and make a good first impression. Follow the interviewer's lead. Answer questions positively. Get the interviewer's name and address.

Prewriting

Sample answers for graphic organizer:

Center oval for main idea: Thank you for taking time to interview me.

Details in outer ovals: My experience will enable me to learn the job quickly. I relate well with customers. I've always wanted to work for your company.

Write a draft.

The first draft should use proper form for a business letter. It should thank the interviewer and explain why you want the job and would be a good fit for it.

Revise and create a final draft.

The final draft should include a leading sentence that sums up the main point of the letter. It should also include details to support that main idea (the thank-you). The letter should be written with correct form, grammar, and word usage.

Lesson 3 The Stepfamily
pp. 25–34

Writing Sentences

Sample answers:

1. I spoke <u>defiantly</u> when my father asked why I was late.

2. I feel <u>exasperation</u> when my friend won't stop talking.

3. Because she was on the phone, my sister <u>ignored</u> me when I was talking to her.

4. When you do something <u>wearily</u>, you feel tired.

5. People speak <u>hesitantly</u> when they are uncertain.

Sentence Completions

1. reconciliation

2. prompted

3. defiantly

4. determined

5. hesitantly

Word Building

Sample answers:

2. promptly: in a prompt way; Jim arrived promptly at noon.

3. fondly: in a fond way; I remember my first love fondly.

4. eagerly: in an eager way; We eagerly awaited her return.

5. calmly: in a calm way; Sarah spoke calmly about the accident.

Writing Activity

Answers will vary. Review the vocabulary words and the definitions. Find the words in the story to see how they are used.

Check your comprehension.

Sample answers:

1. Doris gets angry at Gilly because Gilly's room is such a mess.

2. Gilly tells her father Doris was with another man to make him angry with Doris.

3. Doris can't act as a parent to Gilly.

4. Franco knows the family is getting along better because Gilly asked Doris to go shopping with her.

Compare and contrast.

Sample answers:

Left oval: Gilly is Franco's daughter, is younger than Doris

Middle oval: Gilly and Doris are female, love Franco, are angry

Right oval: Doris is Franco's wife, is older than Gilly

Use a graphic organizer.

Sample answers:

At the beginning of the story: Gilly and Doris are fighting. Franco is ignoring the situation.

At the end of the story: Gilly and Doris are getting along better. Franco is more involved.

Prewriting

Sample answer:

The problem: My friend argues with her husband all the time.

What caused the problem: Her husband goes out with friends after work and doesn't come home until late. She is home alone and gets angry with him.

Has the problem been resolved: Yes, things are better now. He does not go out with his friends as often. When he does go out, his wife sometimes joins him and his friends.

Thinking Beyond Reading

The graphic organizer might now include more about how the family members felt.

Write a draft.

Base your writing on the graphic organizer you filled out on page 33.

Revise and create a final draft.

The final draft should begin by stating the problem. The concluding sentence should tell how the family resolved their problem or how the people are feeling now. Check your final draft for grammar and usage errors.

Lesson 4 Living in a Community
pp. 35–44

Writing Sentences

Sample answers:

1. Jamal is <u>fuming</u> because someone threw a bottle at him.

2. I know Tonya is an <u>enthusiastic</u> gardener because she keeps talking about it.

3. Lakeesha feels <u>overwhelmed</u> because Tonya gives her so much information.

4. I have had <u>doubt</u> about our project when it looked like no one supported it.

5. The storm was so <u>forceful</u> that it blew a tree down onto my car.

Sentence Completions

1. overwhelmed

2. vacant

3. frowned

4. discouraging

5. dismay *or* irritation

Word Building

Sample answers:

2. full of stress; That was a stressful meeting.

3. without use; This tool is useless!

4. state of being kind; She always treats people with kindness.

Writing Activity

Answers will vary. Review the vocabulary words and the definitions. Find the words in the story to see how they are used.

Check your comprehension.

Sample answers:

1. Tonya loves community gardens.

2. Lakeesha and Jamal go to the company that owns the lot to get the OK to make the garden.

3. The neighbors help out.

Identify cause and effect.

Sample answers:

1. *Cause:* Tonya works in the garden.

2. *Effect:* Tonya gets some of the vegetables.

Use a graphic organizer.

Sample answers:

1. *Effect:* They learn how to make a garden.

2. *Cause:* They plant vegetable seeds and take care of them.

Prewriting

Answers will vary but should include a series of steps (causes and their effects) that helped someone.

Thinking Beyond Reading

The graphic organizer should include a clear description of the causes and effects of your actions.

Write a draft.

The first draft should include the information in the graphic organizer. Explain your actions and describe the causes and effects of doing something that made you proud.

Revise and create a final draft.

The final draft should include a topic sentence that tells the main idea of the narrative. Then it should clearly explain what happened and why it happened.

Lesson 5 Learn a Trade
pp. 45–54

Writing Sentences

Sample answers:

1. I have a driver's <u>license</u>.

2. Child care and data entry are popular <u>professions</u>.

3. A person in an <u>administrative</u> job files papers.

4. Teaching is a <u>specific</u> career I'm interested in.

5. Nurse's aide is a job <u>related</u> to health care.

Sentence Completions

1. tuition

2. reputation

3. available

4. enroll

5. connections

Word Building

Circle –*er* or –*ier* at the end of each word.

Sample answers:

2. prettier: The tulip is prettier than the rose.

3. heavier: A rock is heavier than a pebble.

4. darker: The sky is darker tonight than it was last night.

Writing Activity

Answers will vary. Review the vocabulary words and the definitions. Find the words in the article to make sure they are used correctly.

Check your comprehension.

Sample answers:

1. Trade schools are different from colleges because they train people for specific jobs.

2. Those schools may not help you get a job or have qualified teachers. They may not have many company connections or up-to-date equipment.

3. If a school is accredited, it is in good standing with the state.

4. You should expect to do some bookwork and some hands-on work in a trade school.

Make inferences.

Sample answers:

2. Not all the people who finish trade school get jobs.

3. Some schools have complaints filed against them.

Use a graphic organizer.

Sample answers:

1. Comparing shows how things are different.

2. Not all trade schools are the same.

3. I want to be an electrician.

4. I should think about going to a trade school.

Prewriting

Answers will vary, but should include the main idea that the right trade school can help you learn the skills you need for a job you want. Supporting details include seeing if a trade school will give you the education you need, looking carefully at the school and comparing it with others, or looking at several ways to pay for trade school.

Thinking Beyond Reading

The graphic organizer might now include how to decide if you should go to a trade school, how to choose one, or why some schools are better than others.

Write a draft.

The first draft should include the main idea and supporting details from the graphic organizer on page 53.

Revise and create a final draft.

The final draft should begin with a topic sentence that sums up the main idea of the paragraph. The final draft should have few grammatical and usage errors.

Lesson 6 Trial by Jury
pp. 55–64

Writing Sentences

Sample answers:

1. An <u>attorney</u> defends people charged with a crime.

2. If you <u>testify</u>, you tell the court what happened.

3. A <u>unanimous</u> decision is one everyone agrees with.

4. An animal that behaves <u>viciously</u> often attacks violently.

Sentence Completions

1. testimony

2. thoroughly

3. innocent

4. witness

Word Building

Circle *movie, juri (jury), case.*

Sample answers:

2. boxes: I opened the boxes as soon as I got home.

3. lawyers: Good lawyers are very helpful to their clients.

4. injuries: The jury talked about Janice's injuries.

Writing Activity

Answers will vary. Review the vocabulary words and the definitions. Find the words in the paragraph to make sure they are used correctly.

Check your comprehension.

Sample answers:

1. The prosecution says Kevin Macon killed his girlfriend because he was violent and jealous.

2. The next-door neighbor says that Kevin Macon is a person who hit Janice and yelled at her.

3. Kaycee thought the jury foreman seemed fair.

4. The jury found Kevin Macon guilty of murder.

Synthesize information.

Sample answers:

The process of being chosen for a jury begins when a jury summons arrives in the mail. People come to court, are chosen by number to be interviewed, and jury members are selected.

Use a graphic organizer.

Sample answers:

In boxes: jury listens to testimony; jury talks about evidence; jury reaches a decision; jury tells decision to court.

Synthesis: A jury is chosen, listens to all the evidence, and reaches a verdict based on what the jury members think of the evidence.

Prewriting

Answers will vary. Ovals might include these pieces of information: marks on Janice are proof Kevin was violent, Janice asked Kevin if he was going to kill her, the other boyfriend was also violent, no other boyfriend appeared on the stand.

Synthesis: After carefully considering all the evidence, the jury decided that Kevin was guilty beyond a reasonable doubt.

Thinking Beyond Reading

The graphic organizer might now include more information on which to base the synthesis, such as no evidence directly tied Kevin to the crime; Kevin had a violent past and hurt Janice.

Write a draft.

The first draft should include the main points written in the graphic organizer.

Revise and create a final draft.

The final draft should begin with a topic sentence that sums up the main point of the explanation. The final draft should have few grammatical and usage errors.

Lesson 7 Staying Fit
pp. 65–74

Writing Sentences

Sample answers:

1. A <u>disabled</u> person might not be able to walk.

2. It required <u>exertion</u> to move the furniture in my living room.

3. If I <u>incorporate</u> walking into my life, I might lose weight.

4. A good way to <u>combat</u> feelings of sadness is to walk.

5. My most frequent <u>companions</u> are my children.

Sentence Completions

1. processing

2. gradually

3. effective

4. especially

5. evidence

Word Building

Circle *walk, health.*

Sample answers:

2. happy: happily, unhappy, happier

3. play: replay, plays, playing, playful

4. place: replace, placed, misplace

5. easy: easier, uneasy, easily

Writing Activity

Answers will vary. Review the vocabulary words and the definitions. Find the words in the paragraph to make sure they are used correctly.

Check your comprehension.

Sample answers:

1. Walking may release chemicals that make a person happier.

2. When walking at night, wear light-colored clothes that people can see in the dark.

3. If you can't carry on a conversation, you are walking too fast.

4. A pedometer counts the steps you take.

Make inferences.

Sample answer:

Walking for exercise must be different from ordinary walking.

Use a graphic organizer.

Sample answers:

1. You would have to walk more than a half hour to burn off the calories in one candy bar.

2. People are more likely to be victims of crime at night.

3. Walking at night can be safe if you walk in well-lit places.

Prewriting

Answers will vary, but should include details of what a fitness walk might be like, such as seeing a park as you walk by it, smelling flowers, or hearing people talking.

Thinking Beyond Reading

The graphic organizer might now include more information on what someone taking a fitness walk might see, hear, or smell.

Write a draft.

The first draft should include the main points written in the graphic organizer.

Revise and create a final draft.

The final draft should include a sentence that sums up the main point of the description. Check to make sure your paragraph has few grammar and usage errors.

Lesson 8 Owning a Home, Losing a Home pp. 75–84

Writing Sentences

Sample answers:

1. <u>Eventually</u>, I will finish school.

2. My car and my clothes are some of my <u>possessions</u>.

3. I <u>reduced</u> my spending by eating at home more often.

4. A chair that is <u>rickety</u> isn't very strong.

5. I felt <u>despair</u> when I lost my job.

Sentence Completions

1. misery

2. expiration

3. proceedings

4. reassuring

5. subdued

Word Building

Circle *un-, pre-, post-, un-*

Sample answers:

2. before history was written; He found some prehistoric bones.

3. after war; There was a huge postwar celebration.

4. not happy; The unhappy woman sat staring at the rain.

Writing Activity

Answers will vary. Review the vocabulary words and the definitions. Find the words in the paragraph to make sure they are used correctly.

Check your comprehension.

Sample answers:

1. Joyce had to leave her job because she hurt her back.

2. Joyce threw out the bills because she felt it was no use looking at them since she couldn't pay them.

3. The man from the bank told Joyce that the bank was going to foreclose so she would have to leave the house.

Make judgments.

Sample answer:

My judgment is that Joyce should never have gotten on the ladder because an unsteady ladder means that you might fall.

Use a graphic organizer.

Sample answers:

1. Joyce is not being smart because she might be able to keep her house if she talks to her creditors and to the bank.

2. Joyce's kids might have been less upset if they had known why she was unhappy. They might have been able to help in some way.

Prewriting

Answers will vary, but should note what foreclosure is and why it happens. The graphic organizer should also note things to do to avoid foreclosure, such as talking to the bank or selling the house.

Thinking Beyond Reading

Add new ideas to your graphic organizer.

Write a draft.

Your first draft might begin by summing up the main point of the letter. Include the supporting points you wrote in your graphic organizer.

Revise and create a final draft.

The final draft should have few grammatical, usage, and spelling errors.